BUSES

YEARBOOK 2017

Edited by STEWART J. BROWN

KEY PUBLISHING

BUSES
YEARBOOK 2017

FRONT COVER: **The current range of stylish double-deckers - a topic addressed by Gavin Booth - is illustrated by a Wrightbus StreetDeck for First's Worcester fleet.** ALAN MILLAR

BACK COVER (UPPER): **The latest Enviro400 MMC body has been built on Volvo B5LH hybrid chassis. This 2015 Stagecoach London example is in Greenwich in 2015.** GAVIN BOOTH

BACK COVER (LOWER): **A Cityrider Optare Versa in Plumline livery seen in Hanley with D&G Bus in September 2015.** CLIFF BEETON

PREVIOUS PAGE: **Eastern National received 20 Dennis Darts with Plaxton Pointer bodies in 1994. A number are parked in Colchester Bus Station.** GEOFF MILLS

Published by Key Publishing Ltd.
www.keypublishing.com

First Published July 2016

ISBN: 978-1-910415-62-7

Printed by
Gomer Press Ltd
Llandysul Enterprise Park
Llandysul
Ceredigion
SA44 4JL

www.busesmag.com

Fondly remembered old friends

Many of the independent local bus operators that appeared to thrive before deregulation in 1986 have disappeared. *Buses* editor **ALAN MILLAR** looks back at some of those in various parts of England.

Pre-October 1986, when the bus industry was regulated and dominated by public sector operators, independents occupied a special place in many of our hearts.

Not necessarily every one, but certainly the diminishing number that ran stage carriage routes — local bus services today — and especially if they ran them with double-deckers. Even more if their networks were large enough to justify route numbers and buses with fleetnumbers.

The best of these ran fleets that were bought new or offered a mix of new and secondhand purchases that might include manufacturers' ex-demonstrators and development vehicles. Although many were careful in their selection of what they operated, some found it hard to resist a bargain. A low mileage vehicle sold out of a big fleet would be worth a try, even if subsequent experience told them that the big operator had been wise to rid itself of something so troublesome.

The result of all this was an enthusiasts' delight: fleets offering far more variety of chassis and body types than in most major fleets, and often different makes and types than in those major fleets. Better still, they bore liveries peculiar to these operators, often selected to stand apart from any big group or municipal fleet in their area.

We cheered to ourselves when they argued their

A South Notts lowbridge double-decker, a Weymann-bodied Leyland Titan PD3/3, in Nottingham in 1973.

There are as many different reasons why this happened as there were different operators. One, to go back to my second paragraph, is that they were in decline. Family-owned bus companies had been selling out to their larger neighbours since the end of the 1920s when the railways invested capital in the big fleets to help them grow.

Sometimes that was because the owners would have been mad to resist the large sums of money eager buyers were prepared to pay for their businesses. The threats of compulsory nationalisation in the 1950s and coordination in conurbations in the 1960s drove others to sell, as did the steep decline in bus travel that began in the mid-1950s, making it harder to turn a profit especially in rural areas.

So did another inescapable feature of family businesses: that there either was no next generation there to continue a business founded by a father or grandfather, or the next generation had established a viable career in another trade or profession and had no wish to run buses. Or indeed that the family members could not agree about what to do next.

What has also become clear since 1986 is that regulation protected independents as much as the bigger players; they also were part of the status quo. Independents' objections to another operator's expansion plans carried the same weight as those of the big players. And in the pre-1980 regime in which traffic commissioners also regulated fares, many independents were obliged either to charge the same fares as their larger neighbours or raise them at the same time as the big operators, even if their costs were lower.

Deregulation changed all that, and old established independents found themselves under attack from two sides: from big operators no longer restricted to their historic networks; and small, low cost newcomers muscling in on what looked like rich pickings.

way through the traffic courts, overcoming massive opposition from large operators, British Rail, local authorities and others to win traffic commissioners' approval to add new routes to their networks. And we booed to ourselves when they failed in these endeavours, frustrated by a licensing system that favoured those who already held licences and even allowed them to operate the new routes that the independents had proposed and promoted.

So when Nicholas Ridley, the Conservative government's transport secretary from 1983 to 1987, announced that road service licensing for bus services would be abolished and ushered in the Transport Act 1985 to achieve it, there was cause to imagine that this would provide the independents with an opportunity to prosper and grow.

Yet in the 30 years since services were deregulated on 26 October 1986, most of the prominent independent local bus operators have disappeared, most of their routes swallowed into the big private sector groups that bought the public sector fleets. A tiny handful survives and some newcomers have also prospered to stay the course, but the classic independent stage carriage businesses that lasted into the 1980s have been among the most prominent victims of the radical change that decade delivered to Britain's buses outside London.

Barton joins Trent

By far the largest independent still running in 1986 was Barton Transport, founded in 1908 and operating over 200 vehicles across the East

Midlands, principally Derbyshire, Nottinghamshire and Leicestershire.

From the perspective of what enthusiasts loved most about an independent, it ticked many boxes. The fleet had all been bought new, was identified by fleetnumbers and the network was large enough to require several garages as well as route numbers. The livery was as distinctive as any of an independent: rich red, maroon and cream with a logo incorporating a flag and a depiction of Robin Hood armed with a bow and arrow.

Fifteen years earlier, the fleet had ticked more boxes than any bus admirer should have expected to see. It was an extraordinary mix of double- and single-deckers bought new and secondhand, some of them heavily rebuilt and rebodied.

The double-deckers bought new were lowbridge vehicles built to its own specification, mostly with Northern Counties bodies finished with full-width fronts and wrap-round glazing; the last had arrived in 1963. Many of the single-deckers were coaches capable of operating heavily peaked seasonal coach services to places like the Lincolnshire coast in the summer and stage carriage routes in winter.

That changed in the early 1970s as Barton — like other independents — took advantage of the New Bus Grant scheme that lasted from 1968 to 1984 and saw taxpayers fund up to half the cost of new vehicles. New Bus Grant was meant to accelerate the introduction of driver-only operation, but was paid for any vehicle that met the necessary requirements and was used primarily on stage carriage routes, even if that vehicle replaced one already staffed only by a driver.

It spawned the 'grant coach', with a wider entrance and other necessities for local bus operation, and Barton bought them with a vengeance, replacing almost its entire fleet in 1972-76 with Plaxton-bodied Leyland Leopards and Bedfords capable of operating every route in its diverse network. By 1989, at least half the fleet dated from that period of state-subsidised investment and needed to be replaced.

This was not the only state involvement in Barton, as the National Bus Company had a small shareholding in the business, which it sold back to the Barton family when NBC was preparing its own subsidiaries for sale.

The company was struggling, however. Deregulation of coach services in 1980 had opened that part of the business to competition and the bus routes were losing money. The management team that bought Trent from NBC in December 1986 made several approaches to buy Barton and in July 1989

Premier Travel bought some 10-year-old AEC/Park Royal Bridgemasters from City of Oxford Motor Services in 1972. This is Drummer Street bus station in Cambridge the following summer, with coach passengers waiting with suitcases while one of the company's travel agencies is in the building on the left.

In its latter years as an independent, Whippet traded as Go Whippet. This 2011 view shows a Northern Counties-bodied Volvo Citybus, new to Whippet 22 years earlier, crossing the River Cam near Cambridge city centre.

An Alexander Dennis Enviro400 supplied new to Hedingham in 2007 in Saffron Walden two years later.

agreed a £2million deal to acquire its vehicles and routes.

What the Trent team discovered after buying the business was probably little different from the way many independents worked, only on a larger scale. When I interviewed Trent's chairman, Brian King, in 1991, he spelt out the challenges, which bear repeating.

'[Barton] was an organisation which had never been institutionalised. We inherited a traffic superintendent and an engineer, who was a family member. Only the traffic superintendent survived. Otherwise, there was a paucity of management.

'There had been no cross-fertilisation of ideas with other bus companies and no influx of experience with managers other than those home grown. That's been a traditional strength of much of the larger industry.

'Symptoms of Barton's problems were insufficient focus on the profitable parts of the business and an absence of identification of those parts. There was no structure to control all the staff, which meant that there was a friendly, but costly paternalism. It was not a cheap company to run.

'There was very lax labour control. If staff failed to achieve what they wanted by talking to their superiors, they usually got it by a direct approach on the spot to the family.'

To begin with, King and his colleagues kept Barton as a separate brand, sharing overheads with Trent but with operating quirks and staff terms and conditions of its own, but in 2002 it combined them to trade as Trent Barton, Trentbarton or even trentbarton if you can live with uncapitalised proper

nouns. Most of its routes have brands of their own, so although the Barton name survives, on most buses it is a small part of the name that supports brands like Rapid, Swift, Rainbow and The Threes.

In January 2012 it acquired another pre-deregulation independent, Felix of Stanley, which had been operating between Derby and Ilkeston since 1921, latterly in joint operation with Trent Barton.

South Notts and Gash

Another high profile East Midlands independent to lose its independence was South Notts, based in the village of Gotham (pronounced Goat'um) between Nottingham and Loughborough. It had been running since 1926, and from 1927 had been 50% owned by Barton as part of a deal to end competition between the two firms.

Barton appeared to treat the relationship more as an investment, for there was nothing remotely Barton-like about its fleet of 25 to 30 vehicles. The Dabell family ran it throughout its existence, mainly with double-deckers from the 1950s and with a livery of dark blue, maroon and cream. It used fleetnumbers and route numbers.

It had expanded in 1952, winning a traffic court battle to secure 25% of the services to the large Clifton estate being built on the southern edge of Nottingham, operating there in addition to its main route between Loughborough and Nottingham, which passed through Clifton.

South Notts needed lowheight double-deckers, for many years because of a low bridge on the main route and throughout its existence because its depot could accommodate nothing higher. It liked Leylands and was notable in buying five Albion-built Lowlanders in the 1960s, then Atlanteans, Fleetlines (the last two had the last Fleetline chassis built) and finally two Olympians in 1989/90.

It entered the deregulated era with some modest gains of tendered services, but came under attack from May 1990 when Kinch, a Loughborough coach operator expanding into bus operation, began competing between Clifton and Nottingham, later between Nottingham and Loughborough.

Fearing that Kinch might then buy South Notts, council-owned Nottingham City Transport — which also was under attack from the newcomer — bought South Notts in January 1991. It kept its identity and depot — the livery had been simplified in latter years to drop maroon — and when NCT put new Alexander Dennis Enviro400-bodied Scanias on to the Loughborough route in 2015, they were branded Navy Line 1 and painted two-tone blue with a red South Notts name in traditional underlined capital letters.

Sadly, no such fate met the other independent that had run into Nottingham for nearly as many decades as South Notts. W. Gash & Sons had been carrying passengers since 1919 and from 1932 operated into the city from Newark, where it was based from 1953. It earned its place in the enthusiast firmament by running exposed radiator Daimler CVD6 double-

OK Motor Services bought many of its vehicles secondhand. This AEC Regent V with Metro-Cammell body had been built for Halifax in 1960.
ERIC HUTCHINSON

deckers into the mid-1970s long after such delights had disappeared elsewhere, by maintaining a livery of dark turquoise, pale green and cream and using alphanumerical fleetnumbers.

Come deregulation, it expanded by winning contracts for tendered services and added secondhand double-deckers. It overstretched itself and in April 1988 sold out to Traction Group, which three months earlier had bought Lincolnshire Road Car from NBC.

The intention was to keep it going as a separate business, but maintenance problems led to the operator licence being revoked and it was absorbed into Road Car, whose vehicle authorisation was increased accordingly. Road Car kept one of the old Daimlers for a while, but Gash's latter years had tainted the name too much to keep the name.

Its spirit lives on, however, as John Marshall, a part-time driver with Gash, set up on his own in Sutton-on-Trent in 1989, painting his growing fleet — several have been bought new — blue and cream and giving them alphanumerical fleetnumbers in Gash style. It may be Marshalls rather than Gash, but is the next best thing.

The rollercoaster that was Stevensons
Stevensons of Uttoxeter — based in the nearby village of Spath — started operating in 1926 between Uttoxeter and Burton-upon-Trent, ran six routes by 1939 and had grown to a fleet of 28 by 1961. It had fleetnumbers, route numbers and a distinctive livery of yellow, white and black with a fleetname displayed around a rising sun.

That could easily have been the end of the Stevensons story, for after the founder's death in 1966 most of the family wanted to sell up. Two of his sons did not and the disagreement may explain why neither of the area's big group operators — Trent and Potteries Motor Traction — chose to buy it. The impasse took five years to settle and ended with one of the sons buying it back in a public auction.

By 1980, it had 47 vehicles, mostly schoolbuses and coaches, but over the next 14 years it expanded to 270 bought new and secondhand and spanning the East and West Midlands, as well as having interests in businesses in south Wales and eastern Scotland. Its story typifies the rollercoaster first years of deregulation.

It was in 1980 that a young transport management graduate called Julian Peddle joined as traffic manager; three years later he owned half the business and became its managing director.

Under Peddle's management, Stevensons exploited opportunities to expand, starting by extending the original Uttoxeter-Burton route into Burton town centre from the outlying bus station where out-of-town operators had been required to decant their passengers on to municipal buses. It plugged gaps that opened up when NBC companies started rationalising their networks as they implemented Market Analysis Project reviews, and bought up a couple of other operators to develop more routes.

As Ridley's Transport Act loomed on the horizon in 1985, it struck a remarkable deal, taking over the loss-making 38-vehicle East Staffordshire municipal undertaking in Burton in return for the council taking a 50% stake in the enlarged business. This saved the council from setting up an arm's length company the next year, which the new legislation demanded, a company that would likely have struggled to survive against the area's ex-NBC operators.

Like many operators in the early 1980s, Stevensons took advantage of London Transport's premature disposal of DMS-class Fleetlines, available from the Ensign dealership for about £5,000 each. It used

DMSs to replace 18 expensive-to-maintain Dennis Dominators inherited from East Staffordshire and radically altered the Burton network to increase frequencies, gain extra passengers and use just 18 vehicles.

Stevensons was one of three bidders shortlisted to buy Midland Fox — the eastern part of Midland Red — from NBC. The Fox management team was another of the three and they came together in a deal in August 1987 that saw Stevensons take a 33% share in Fox and acquire the Fox depots in Swadlincote and Lichfield.

Stevensons used Lichfield as a springboard to expand into the lucrative West Midlands market, eventually running 140 buses there. However, that proved a thorn in the side of West Midlands Travel, which hit back on Stevensons' routes in Sutton Coldfield and the Black Country, and — when Stevensons declined to rush into a joint venture with it — registered competing services in Burton.

This unsettled East Staffordshire council into seeking a buyer for its share in Stevensons. WMT wanted to buy, but that was Stevensons' least favoured option. Instead, British Bus, which in its previous incarnation as Drawlane had bought Midland Fox in 1989, acquired the entire share capital in Stevensons in June 1994.

It retained its separate identity until the Arriva brand was introduced in 1997 and Stevensons of

Uttoxeter survived as the legal owner of some Arriva Midlands buses until 2015, but its days as a thrusting independent were long over. In 2016, however, Arriva sold the Burton operation to Midland Classic, a post-deregulation independent in which Julian Peddle has a financial interest.

In north Staffordshire, Berresford Motors of Cheddleton closed in 1987 and the privatised PMT company acquired Turner's of Brown Edge in 1988.

Premier, like Barton but blue

The smaller East Anglian equivalent of Barton was Premier Travel, based in Cambridge and operating a mix of local bus routes and long distance coach services, its buses painted blue and cream, its coaches two-tone blue. It used fleetnumbers and route numbers.

It was founded in January 1936 by Arthur Lainson, a young Cambridge graduate with a passion for bus and coach operation (he was an early member of the Omnibus Society) and a vision to operate scheduled long-distance coach services.

He and nine fellow students had already indulged in coach operation before graduating and he possessed the powers of persuasion and social connections of a man educated at a top university and before that at Harrow school. Besides acquiring two local operators, he also secured funding for the venture from the knighted former director of the Premier Omnibus Company, compulsorily acquired by London Transport in 1933, who became the company's first chairman.

It started with six vehicles, but by the mid-1960s had over 50 operating mainly from Cambridge and the London overspill town of Haverhill in Suffolk. Lainson achieved his ambition in long distance coach operation with cross-country routes that stretched eventually from Scotland and the north of England to the Essex, Suffolk, Norfolk and Lincolnshire coasts, as well as to Oxford and the London airports. Some of the coach services — many were seasonal — ran jointly with other operators including Yelloway of Rochdale and NBC.

While it bought new coaches — from 1965 to 1974 it was one of few independents buying Alexander Y-type bodies (on AEC Reliance chassis) — the buses (some double-deck) were usually secondhand and the business weathered several financial crises that likely would have sunk equivalent companies today when banks show a lot less discretion towards clients running low on cash. There were tales of conductors being instructed to pay their takings straight into the bank to stave off disaster during difficult times.

Premier survived the deregulation of coach services in 1980, but bus deregulation brought new threats to a route network that declined as rural populations changed and car ownership grew. Many required subsidies and were opened up to competitive tendering, while commercial routes around Cambridge were potentially in competition with Cambus, the local NBC subsidiary sold to its management at the end of 1986.

By then, 89% of Premier's earnings came from its travel agencies rather than buses and coaches, and the business was offered for sale in December 1987. The travel agency went in a management buyout and it looked initially that Cambus would get the buses and coaches until a last minute deal saw the AJS Group — headed by former East Yorkshire Motor Services managing director Alan Stephenson — step in and keep it intact.

The new owner invested in minibuses to compete against Cambus in Haverhill and Royston, with the threat of more routes to come in Cambridge, and also developed new big bus routes, but in May 1990 AJS sold most of the Premier operation — local buses, National Express and private hire coaches — to Cambus, which made Premier its coach division.

AJS kept a rump of other long distance coach work — mainly the growing and highly profitable routes to the London airports — as Cambridge Coach Services, selling this on to the Blazefield management buy-out that acquired AJS's other ex-NBC operations. Blazefield expanded the CCS network before selling it to National Express in October 1999.

Whippet, Hedingham and Chambers

In 1947 and 1951, Premier had discussed a possible takeover of Whippet Coaches, but nothing came of these and Whippet — founded in 1919 and with routes serving Cambridge, Huntingdon, St Ives and St Neots — remained in the ownership of the Lee family until November 2014.

It started in the village of Graveley in what then was Huntingdonshire, moved to nearby Hilton, then Fenstanton and finally to Swavesey in 2009. It bought its first new vehicle in 1930, its first double-decker in 1955 and its first new double-decker in 1966.

By 1976, the fleet — painted blue and cream — had grown to 36 and post-deregulation expansion took it to around 60 buses and coaches, some of the latter working for National Express. Most of its double-deckers were acquired secondhand, although it often bought batches of similar vehicles and between 1982 and 1992 acquired 28 Scania/MCW Metropolitans, 17 of which had been new to London Transport.

It sold the Fenstanton base to Stagecoach, which uses it as the base for guided buses operated on the Cambridge-St Ives Busway, but Whippet also won rights to operate on the Busway, for which it bought new Volvo B7RLE single-deckers.

Its presence on the Busway probably made the business more attractive to purchasers and when the third generation of Lees had no fourth generation willing to continue running Whippet, they sold it to a family-owned business on the other side of the world. It became a subsidiary of Tower Transit, the London division of Australian-owned Transit Systems.

Nearly two years on, Whippet retains its distinct identity, albeit in a new style, the fleet updated with the transfer of mid-life double-deckers from London. It already used route numbers and new ownership has given the fleet alphanumeric fleetnumbers a little like those in London.

Elsewhere in East Anglia, Hedingham Omnibuses remained independent for nearly 26 years after deregulation.

It had begun life in 1921 in the Essex village of Sible Hedingham, founded by Aubrey Letch in whose name it traded until Donald MacGregor acquired it in 1960 and changed the name to Hedingham & District Omnibuses. It had eight vehicles then, all with fleetnumbers prefixed by L for Letch and in the MacGregor family's ownership it continued that fleetnumbering sequence into the L380s.

It grew by a series of acquisitions, most notably of Osborne's of Tollesbury in 1997, and by March 2012 had 86 red and cream buses — many bought new — at five depots in Essex and Suffolk on a mix of commercial and tendered bus services, school contracts and registered school routes.

It was acquired then by Go-Ahead Group, which two years earlier had embarked on an expansion into Norfolk and Suffolk by purchasing Konectbus, a post-deregulation new start independent. Hedingham took it farther south and initially very little changed, with founder's son Robert MacGregor remaining in charge.

Three months later, Go-Ahead bought Chambers of Bures, which had been serving rural Essex and Suffolk for 140 years and was one of the last local bus operators in the country still running no low-floor vehicles.

Chambers's 30 vehicles transferred to Hedingham's Sudbury depot, retaining their separate identity.

Turning family-owned independents into PLC group subsidiaries is a challenge and Go-Ahead eventually installed a new management team at Hedingham and Chambers, rebalanced the work to do more commercial routes and fewer tendered contracts, adopted a new livery of two-tone red (the darker shade a nod to Chambers), cascaded many vehicles in from other group fleets (mainly London) and replaced Hedingham's L-prefixed fleetnumbers with a new combined series for East Anglia.

In Buckinghamshire, Red Rover of Aylesbury sold out to employee-owned Luton & District in 1987. In Surrey, the 77-year-old Tillingbourne company, which had expanded into a 70-vehicle operation with routes into Berkshire, collapsed in March 2001. And in rural Dorset, Bere Regis & District, founded in 1929, sold the bulk of its operations in March 1994 to Southern National owner Cawlett, which renamed it Dorchester Coachways

Not so OK up north

The casualty list in the north of England has been formidable. The biggest was the Emerson family's OK Travel, which as OK Motor Services was a prominent part of the north-east bus scene from shortly after World War 1, with routes radiating from its base in Bishop Auckland as far as Newcastle and a livery of two-tone red and cream.

It ran double-deckers from 1946 and 30 years later had nearly 60 vehicles, half of them coaches. It seized the expansion opportunity presented by deregulation, opening a new depot in Peterlee, and by the early 1990s was running nearly 200 vehicles, most purchased secondhand.

Competition with what then was Go-Ahead Northern intensified in 1994 into a full-scale bus war with tit-for-tat registrations. Although the battle ended that summer, OK was over-stretched and in a poor financial state, and the family was keen to sell. Go-Ahead acquired it in March 1995 and within three years had sold off the coach side and absorbed the bus operations into its existing business. It abandoned Bishop Auckland to Arriva in 2006.

OK outlasted Trimdon Motor Services (TMS), which had traded as a partnership for four years when it became a limited company in 1929 and by the 1970s was running nearly 50 blue buses across Co. Durham, with routes to Durham, Bishop Auckland, Hartlepool and Stockton. In new ownership, it introduced secondhand double-deckers to the fleet in 1953, but following its sale to entrepreneur Bob Lewis in

A Northern Counties Paladin-bodied Scania L113CRL supplied new to Mayne's in 1994. SCANIA

1959, it standardised on new single-deckers — Fords initially, later Leyland Leopards and Tigers.

Lewis acquired businesses elsewhere, including Jersey Motor Transport, and judged that TMS's lower operating costs would allow it to compete against the municipal and PTE bus companies in Teesside and Tyneside from 1986. His tools of this new trade were lightweight Bristol LHs, followed by Leopards and Leyland Nationals. All carried TMS's blue and white livery, but on Tyneside it traded as the Tyne & Wear Omnibus Company (TWOC).

But with Lewis turning 65 at the end of 1989, he wanted to sell the business rather than pass it on to a younger generation. TWOC went first, in November 1989, sold to Go-Ahead, which sold it on immediately — much to Lewis's annoyance — to Busways, the management-owned former PTE company that shut it all down three months later.

He sold TMS in March 1990 to Caldaire Holdings, the West Riding management team that had bought

United Auto from NBC. The Teesside operations continued, but the original TMS closed after six months, amalgamated into United.

During the 1970s, South Yorkshire PTE bought up most of the independents running daily services into Doncaster from surrounding mining communities. Its successor, South Yorkshire Transport, acquired the 13-vehicle two-tone blue and cream Premier of Stainforth in June 1988, but Leon Motor Services of Finningley survived into the 21st century.

Leon had been operating since 1928 and painted its fleet sea green and cream, adorning them with fleetnumbers. MASS Engineering, which still operates Brightbus-branded green double-deck schoolbuses today, acquired Leon in February 2004, but closed it in September 2007 when First South Yorkshire — the privatised incarnation of SYT — took over its three services.

Not to be confused with SYT was South Yorkshire Road Transport, a Pontefract-based independent with routes stretching out to Leeds and Doncaster. It had been around since 1929 and until 1973 was called South Yorkshire Motors.

A 16-year-old Northern Counties Paladin-bodied
Dennis Dart of Pennine operating a Skipton town
service in 2011.

It had the appearance of a business that might
operate more than its actual fleet of 18 vehicles,
painting them two-tone blue and cream until 1973,
then in a professionally designed two-tone blue and
white livery with big SY logos. All its vehicles were
bought new, including Northern Counties-bodied
Leyland Olympians purchased post deregulation.

Caldaire bought the business in July 1994, adapting
the livery into a blue version of the green and cream
and red and cream schemes applied to its West
Riding and Yorkshire Woollen fleets.

The brand did not last long, for Caldaire was
acquired by British Bus in March 1995, then in
June 1996 the Cowie group acquired British Bus,
rebranding itself in late 1997 as Arriva with a
national livery that swept away all that lay before
it, including the last traces of South Yorkshire Road
Transport.

Mayne's, Pennine and Fishwick's

Three particularly fondly followed independents
have gone from north-west England. The first was
Mayne's of Manchester, which survives as a coach
business in Warrington but sold its 38-vehicle bus
operation to Stagecoach in January 2008.

It began running buses in 1923 and was a rare
example of a pre-1986 independent operating
into the heart of a major city centre. By 1975, it
operated nine maroon and turquoise AEC Regent V

double-deckers on route 213 along the Ashton New
Road between Droylsden and Stevenson Square in
Manchester.

Manchester Corporation made several attempts to
buy the business but instead arranged for Mayne's
to operate the 213 on its behalf. This arrangement
survived after Selnec PTE took over the municipal
fleets in 1969 and continued under Greater
Manchester PTE until deregulation in 1986. It was
highly advantageous to Mayne's, which passed the
fares revenue to the PTE in return for a rate per
mile based on the PTE's running costs, which were
around double those of Mayne's.

While that apparent goldmine was exhausted in
October 1986, Mayne's expanded its bus operations,
buying new and secondhand vehicles — and painting
them in a new livery of bright red and cream — to
operate additional commercial routes and compete
for tendered services. By 2000, it had nine core
commercial routes on the Ashton Old and New
Roads, with a 6min service between Droylsden and
Piccadilly in the peaks.

But in stark contrast with the pre-1986 payment
arrangement, Mayne's bus operation recorded a
£1.5million loss in 2005/06 and faced the longer-
term challenge of the Metrolink tram being extended
to Droylsden. The Stagecoach purchase was one of
several of the region's independents at the time.

Although based in North Yorkshire, Pennine Motor
Services tilted more towards Lancashire than its
home county. Its stunning orange, black and grey
livery was inspired by the colours of the Leyland

Motors Football Club and it owed its survival to a close relationship with Ribble, for decades running a joint service between Skipton and Lancaster.

Pennine lasted from Christmas 1925 until May 2014. It was run throughout by three generations of the Simpson family and for most of its existence was based in the village of Gargrave on the A65, close to the Lancashire border, then from 2002 in the former Ribble depot in Skipton.

It bought new Leylands until a troublesome trio of Swift 39-seaters arrived in 1991, then turned to secondhand Leyland Nationals and latterly Dennis Darts. All 14 buses at the end were Darts, some low-floor, on six routes radiating from Skipton to Burnley (the main route, in competition with Transdev), along the A65 to Settle and Giggleswick, and on more local runs.

Other family business interests cross-subsidised Pennine in its later years, but a cut in free concessionary travel remuneration from North Yorkshire County Council was the final straw and the business simply closed down. Transdev and Kirkby Lonsdale Coaches replaced some of the services.

Possibly the most mourned loss of all, in October 2015, came with the closure of Fishwick's of Leyland, whose two-tone green buses served the communities around Leyland, Chorley and Preston from 1911 and which was run by the founder's great grandsons.

It ran 35 vehicles latterly, buses mainly but also a handful of coaches. Until 1992 most of these were locally built Leylands, some of them former demonstrators and development vehicles, and between 1975 and 1981 the manufacturer took advantage of New Bus Grant by supplying eight Leyland Nationals that it then borrowed back from Fishwick's to use as demonstrators.

Eleven buses built between 1968 and 1974 had bespoke bodies constructed in Leyland by W. H. Fowler, a coachbuilder owned by Fishwick's.

In its latter years, Fishwick's sourced a regular supply of new DAF and VDL single-deckers from the Arriva Bus & Coach dealership in West Yorkshire.

Like Pennine, Fishwick's survived through the good grace of Ribble, with which it had a revenue pooling arrangement that lasted from 1935 until October 1986. It faced more competition post deregulation but resisted takeover approaches. In the end, it ran out of cash and was placed in administration. No buyers came forward and Stagecoach — which acquired Ribble in 1989 — replaced the main service between Preston and Leyland.

Independent survival

While these and other long established firms have gone, including in Scotland and Wales, others survive as I write this. Delaine of Bourne, linking small towns of south Lincolnshire with the city of Peterborough, remains firmly in the hands of the fifth and sixth generations of Delaine-Smith family, which has been running motorbuses since 1919.

In Guildford, Safeguard Coaches — founded in 1924 — survives in the ownership of the Newman family, running two town services along with a larger coach business.

Recent developments have also seen First pull out of Hereford, leaving routes in this rural county in independents' hands, the largest of which is Yeomans.

Many big names we have known and loved are no more, but other independents — especially those new to bus operation in the past 30 years — are alive and active. Nothing stands still in the bus world. ∎

The final day of Fishwick's services in October 2015. This three-year-old Wright Pulsar 2-bodied VDL SB200 was typical of the smart condition of this Lancashire fleet throughout its existence.
ANDY RIGBY

All photographs by the author.

The eye of the beholder

Gavin Booth considers the beauty - or otherwise - of double-deck buses.

I like looking at buses. There – I've said it. I don't imagine many readers of this Yearbook will find that odd, but I have friends who do. Friends who spend their weekends shouting at 22 people on a football pitch and don't regard that as odd. Need I say more?

Not only do I like to look at buses, I particularly like to look at double-deckers. And not only that, I like to recognise and identify them. As time goes by, this becomes a bit more difficult – and before you say it, it's not entirely down to the ageing process. I remember a time when I could identify every make and model of private car on Britain's roads, but not now. Of course at that time the vast majority were built at places like Birmingham, Coventry and Oxford. Today the sheer variety of models from all over the world is confusing and some car makers like to maintain a family likeness across their ranges – so I find myself looking at the badges on the tail to confirm if, say, I'm looking at a Jaguar XE, XF or XJ or a Skoda Octavia or Superb.

The Wrightbus Classic single-deck bus range used to cause me some problems – distinguishing an Endurance from a Pathfinder, an Axcess-ultralow, an Axcess Floline, a Liberator and a Renown is not always easy at first glance, particularly when some operators elect not to display model names and chassis makers' logos. What works for the Wrightbus single-deckers is that they are attractive vehicles and look good in the urban streetscape.

There are fewer variations among double-deckers, so that makes life easier, Bodywork identification is pretty simple but there are subtleties like what chassis is the body mounted on? Often the best way is to note which side the rear cooling grille is on – nearside is Alexander Dennis, left is Volvo. I think. Sad, or what?

My working title for this piece was "The good, the bad and the ugly", but I quickly

FirstBus was an enthusiastic customer for the original Wright Gemini; this is a First Aberdeen Volvo B7TL against the backdrop of Marischal College, Aberdeen, in 2014.

The first Alexander low-floor double-deck body was the ALX400, not perhaps the most attractive of the first generation designs. This 2000 First West Yorkshire version on Volvo B7TL chassis – note the offside rear grille – is in Leeds in 2012.

realised that the attention paid to the way buses look means that today there are few bads and even fewer uglies.

Does it really matter what buses look like? There have been times when bus bodybuilders and operators seem to have decided that the answer was "no" and that all buses needed to do was to transport large numbers of people from A to B in a tin box. Which was no doubt fine for the bean-counters trying to balance the books.

Fortunately, there were also visionaries who saw beyond this, who recognised that buses were an essential part of the streetscape in our towns and cities and in the great swathes of countryside in between. People who noticed how much importance car manufacturers placed on the appearance of their products if they were to attract buyers and realised that buses had to look attractive if they were to compete. But of course looks are very subjective – one man's meat, and all that – so what appeals to

me as a passenger and bystander may not cut the mustard with the next man. Or woman. So what I say in the next 1,450 words is very much my take on things and I don't for a second expect you to agree.

The world of course has changed from the one

ABOVE RIGHT: **The Alexander Dennis Enviro400 was introduced in 2005 and was a more attractively rounded design than the ALX400, sold as a complete vehicle with an Alexander-built body on a modified Dennis Trident chassis. This 2007 Transdev Yellow Buses former demonstrator is seen in Bournemouth in 2008.**

BELOW RIGHT: **The latest Enviro400 MMC body has also been built on Volvo B5LH hybrid chassis – note the long rear overhang and, just to confuse us, a nearside radiator grille. This 2015 Stagecoach London example is in Greenwich in 2015.**

many of us grew up with. A time when bus operators had a reasonable selection of chassis makers and a wider range of bodybuilders to choose from. When local authority fleets often gave their business to local firms, a vote-winning move that supported the local economy. And when they didn't, and shopped elsewhere, the local manufacturers sometimes threw their toys out of the pram and shouted "foul!".

Now of course it's a different scenario. If you want to support UK industry, then there is a very limited choice. If you want a UK-built underframe on which to mount a body by your favourite builder, you will be toiling. If you want a complete bus built in the UK, there is no problem, similarly if you want a UK body on an imported chassis. The industry has changed so much, that only the Alexander and Dennis parts of today's Alexander Dennis are really recognisable from the list of builders competing for business more than 40 years ago when we hadn't heard of Optare and Wrights was catering mainly for the Irish market. Today if you want a double-decker for city service your choice is Alexander Dennis, Optare or Wrightbus and, er, that's it. Oh yes – and the Egyptian-built MCV EvoSeti that could yet make an impact in the UK.

And in the days when bus bodies were built rather than assembled, important customers could get bespoke designs that shouted that they were unmistakeably Birmingham or Manchester or Nottingham buses. Not so today, when much of modern bus bodies is built offline and put together on what is essentially an assembly line. This makes sense in terms of build time and if you have developed a structure that has proved pretty indestructible then you stick with that and tweak the bits you can tweak. Unless, of course, you have the clout of Transport for London.

Looking back to the last step-entrance double-deckers, the sharp-edged 1980s look was king until Optare came along with its DAF-based Spectra in 1991 with softer, rounder lines, and two years later Alexander successfully revamped its R type as the more rounded Royale, while Northern Counties did the same to produce the Palatine II. When low-floor double-deckers came along in 1997, Optare got in first with a revamped Spectra, but may have missed a trick because at first glance it didn't look too different from the step-entrance model.

Plaxton, which had acquired Northern Counties in 1995, recognised that low-floor double-deckers

needed to announce to the world that they were different and came up with the President rather than a low-floor Palatine, and showed how attractive these new-generation double-deckers could be. Alexander's ALX400 followed in 1998, with a hint of the Royale about it, but it was arguably the least successful of the first-generation bodies on the low-floor chassis that would quickly render step-entrance buses obsolete.

East Lancs, which had built a long line of solid, well-proportioned double-deck bodies on front-engined chassis for municipal customers, seemed to lose its way with its later bodies on rear-engined chassis, when it offered apparently unlimited permutations on front upstairs peaks or domes, flat or curved glass, gasket or bonded side windows – often with mixed results. East Lancs bodies on low-floor double-deck chassis were better, with deep side windows but a confusing shopping list of type names: Lolyne on Dennis Trident, Vyking on Volvo B7TL, Nordic on three-axle Volvos, OmniDekka on Scania N series and Lowlander on DAF, later VDL, DB250. From 2006 the sharper Olympus became the standard East Lancs double-deck offering, continuing as the Optare Olympus following the 2008 takeover which brought East Lancs and Optare products together under the Optare name.

Optare is still with us in spite of many obstacles that have been placed in its path. From a management buy-out from Leyland Bus, to United Bus, to another management buy-out, to North American Bus Industries, to yet another management buy-out, to Darwen Group, the merger with East Lancs and now Ashok Leyland. All in little more than 30 years.

What Optare brought to the party in 1985 was innovation and good design and in spite of its subsequent ups and downs it still punches above its weight. The 1988 Optare Delta on DAF SB220 chassis proved that single-deck buses could look stylish and less like boxes, and its subsequent string of good-looking buses includes the Solo, Versa and Tempo as well as the Spectra double-decker.

Around the turn of the century it did look like a three-horse race for low-floor double-deck body orders as a result of the acquisitions and mergers, particularly following the creation of the short-lived TransBus International, which brought Alexander, Dennis and Plaxton/Northern Counties under the same ownership, competing for business with East Lancs and Optare. Then Scania decided it would

TOP LEFT: **Optare's low-floor Spectra was broadly similar in looks to the previous step-entrance version, but with deeper lower deck windows and a longer first side window on the upper deck. This 2002 Arriva Yorkshire example is seen in Leeds in 2012.**

BELOW LEFT: **Following its acquisition of the Northern Counties business, Plaxton continued to build double-deck bodies at the Wigan plant. The President was possibly the most attractive of the first-generation low-floor double-deck bodies, and this 2004 Lothian Buses version on TransBus Trident chassis is seen at Port Seton in 2007.**

but I wasn't totally convinced until I saw Geminis in service and recognised how well Wrights had reinvented the shape and essence of the low-floor double-decker.

If I ever had a problem with Wright bodies it was with back ends. The designers at Ballymena clearly recognised that there wasn't much you could do with the sides of a bus, so their main canvas was the front end, which is, after all, what passengers see first. And for a while you had the feeling that nobody actually designed the back ends, which looked as if they were left to a combination of the youngest apprentice and the parts bin. But not today, when Wrightbus back ends actually look as if they belong to the rest of the bus.

More recently Wrightbus has taken weight out of its double-deck bodies by reducing the depth of the upper deck windows and the "Nokia" front end has given way to the much squarer "stealth" look – a bit of a shock at first but one I'm getting used to.

build its own complete OmniCity double-deckers in Poland and for a few years these sold well, with more than 400 bought by London operators alone. And then Wrights entered the fray.

The roots of Wrightbus go back 60 years, but the company hit the big time in the 1990s with orders from the newly-created FirstGroup and its pioneering low-floor single-deck bodies on Dennis and Scania chassis for London Buses. There had been other low-floor buses in the UK before this, but these were imports from Europe, or carried UK-built bodies to Swedish designs.

Then Wrights moved into the double-deck body market with its Gemini. I first saw a Gemini in 2001; it was on the M25 and I was driving in the opposite direction, but I was struck by just how fundamentally different it was from anything else on the market with that heavily arched roofline and the "Nokia" look created by the upper and lower deck windscreens. It was on its way to the UITP display in London where I had a better chance to examine it,

BELOW: **Scania introduced its OmniCity double-deck model in 2005, with Polish-built Scania bodywork, that was essentially its standard single-deck body with the addition of an extra deck, creating a not unattractive bus. This is a 2008 Brighton & Hove example in 2009.**

And, of course, Wrightbus builds the New Routemaster to Thomas Heatherwick's startlingly original design that combines nods to previous generations of London bus with 21st century styling. Even though there are hundreds now in service in London they still make me smile when I see them. Bus design needs a nudge like this every so often – think back to the impact of London Transport's RT design in 1939 – and the influence of the New Routemaster (I nearly typed Borismaster) will filter through to other manufacturers. In fact, it already has with ADL's Enviro400H City, which picks up some cues from the New Routemaster styling and marries these to the existing Enviro400 structure, which itself went through a transformation from the 2005 rounded design to the sharper 2014 snappily-named MMC (Major Model Change) variant. And then there's the SRM, the shorter Wrightbus body on Volvo B5LH chassis, which looks to have a wider appeal outside London than the pure New Routemaster, just as ADL's Enviro400H City has attracted orders.

The New Routemaster is a bit of a Marmite bus – you like it or you hate it, there's no in-between. I must admit to being a fan of virtually everything that that comes out of Wrightbus and Alexander Dennis with very few reservations. I have always admired Optare's flair for design and look forward to seeing if its new Metrodecker can win business from Ballymena and Falkirk. The jury's still out on MCV's EvoSeti, which is more eye-catching than its plainer predecessor, the DD103.

But of course a good livery can disguise fairly mundane body styling, as of course a poor livery can spoil the appearance of a decent-looking bus. Subjectively speaking, of course – but don't get me started on liveries ... ■

TOP RIGHT: **For the East London Transit bus priority measures, Go-Ahead London bought Volvo B9TL with Wrightbus Gemini 2 bodies in 2010 wearing this variation on standard Transport for London livery, seen here when the bus was new.**

BELOW TOP RIGHT: **Wrightbus produced a lowheight version of its Gemini 2 body, creating a squarer and not unattractive look. This is a 2013 Arriva Merseyside version on Volvo B5LH chassis in Liverpool in 2013.**

ABOVE BOTTOM RIGHT: **Most Wrightbus Gemini 3 bodies have been built with the "stealth" upper deck front windows, as here on a Lothian Volvo B5TL seen when new in 2015.**

BOTTOM RIGHT: **Now a familiar sight in London, the Wrightbus New Routemaster; this 2013 example is seen in 2014.**

Following a major fire at its Larkfield garage in 1992 the Strathclyde PTE acquired a number of secondhand buses to replace some of the 60 buses destroyed in the blaze. These included seven East Lancs-bodied Leyland Atlanteans from Nottingham, all of which passed to the GCT business in the autumn of 1993.

Glasgow's GCT

Billy Nicol illustrates a short-lived Glasgow operation.

In August 1993 the newly-privatised Strathclyde Buses – the former PTE business – set up a low-cost subsidiary which traded as GCT, the initials of PTE predecessor Glasgow Corporation Transport. It adopted a yellow and green livery, colours associated with the original GCT and with the PTE, and in the main operated tendered services or routes to compete with some of the smaller operators in the city.

Its initial fleet numbered 50 buses. GCT lasted four years, being wound up in November 1997.

LEFT: **Another source of fire-replacement Atlanteans was Busways of Newcastle-upon-Tyne, whose Alexander-bodied buses did not look out of place in Glasgow, apart from some having a nearside staircase, as on this bus which had been transferred from the main fleet to GCT. It originally had two doors.**

The oldest bus in the GCT fleet was this Atlantean which had been new to the original GCT in 1973 and was repainted in its original livery to mark the centenary of public transport in the city in 1994. It was mainly used on the service linking central Glasgow and the Scottish Exhibition and Conference Centre.

ABOVE: **GCT had a number of MCW Metroriders, most of which were transferred from the parent Strathclyde Buses fleet. This 33-seater dated from 1988.**

ABOVE: **Other Metroriders were acquired from Dublin Bus. A long-wheelbase model is seen in Paisley in 1996.**

LEFT: **The initial GCT fleet included six Alexander-bodied Leyland Olympians purchased from Kelvin Central Buses. This bus had been new to Strathtay Scottish in 1986 and has the characteristic Scottish Bus Group triangular destination layout.**

The first new vehicles for GCT were three East Lancs-bodied Scania K93s. They wore SB Travel coach livery and were used on excursions and private hires.

BELOW: **This coach, acquired from a Maidstone business which used it for staff transport, was a Leyland B43 – a prototype for the Tiger. It had a Duple Dominant body.**

BELOW: **More modern acquisitions, in 1996, included Volvo B6s with Alexander Dash bodies. This was one of a pair of 40-seaters acquired from Allander of Milngavie. They had been new in 1994.**

ABOVE: **The most striking vehicle to wear SB Travel colours was this long-wheelbase Leyland Olympian with ECW coach body. It had been new to London Country Bus Services, but was bought by GCT from Northumbria Motor Services.**

ABOVE: **Strathclyde Buses and GCT were bought by FirstBus in May 1996, and buses in both fleets were repainted dark red, as seen on this freshly-painted Volvo B10M with Alexander PS-type body. The bus was new to Stagecoach Glasgow.**

Towards the end of GCT operations eight Dennis Dart SLFs with East Lancs Spryte bodies were purchased, and these were delivered in First's unrelieved red. This bus is seen in Clydebank in 1997.

The rise and fall of Cityrider

A council-owned bus fleet helped support unremunerative services in and around Stoke-on-Trent. **Cliff Beeton** charts its history.

S ocially-necessary bus services in Stoke-on-Trent after local bus deregulation in 1986 were subsidised by Stoke-on-Trent City Council. They tended to be operated mainly by old second-hand step-entrance minibuses. Although cheap and reliable to run, they were hardly ideal for the people who tended to rely on these services who were mainly elderly or else young parents with children and associated prams, pushchairs and shopping trolleys.

In the late 1990s low-floor buses were starting to appear in many major bus fleets nationwide, mainly being used on the premium commercial routes that made the most profit for their operators. In 2000 the city council was keen to see users of socially-necessary bus services also benefitting from modern low-floor, fully-accessible vehicles, but unless the tender prices rose significantly, it was unlikely that

ABOVE: **The first vehicle for Cityrider was D&G-operated Dennis Dart DA51 XTC, seen here posed for a photograph the day after delivery in the car park opposite the then D&G Bus garage at Longton in February 2001.**

local independent operators would be able to afford to buy these vehicles for services that would never be commercially viable.

A novel solution by the council was to launch Cityrider, a scheme whereby the council would fund the purchase of brand new accessible buses. They would be funded by a government grant as part of Local Transport Plan, and the council would then

RIGHT: **Wardle Transport operated three Optare Aleros on demand-responsive routes 898 and 899, which were marketed as Cityrider on Call. YP52 BPF waits at Bradeley Village in December 2002. The temperamental Aleros were soon replaced by Optare Solos.**

allocate the buses to the operator who had won the tender. The tender price would reflect the fact that the vehicles were being provided. By the council.

The scheme would benefit the smaller independent operators as they would not have to spend large sums of money up front investing in new vehicles. The operator would, however, still be responsible for taxing, insuring and maintaining them. A bright livery of red, white and blue was chosen with prominent Stoke-on-Trent logo and Cityrider fleetname. Operators would be allowed to add their own fleetnumbers to the vehicles, and to apply their fleetnames. At the end of any contract, the buses would have to be handed over to the succeeding operator in "as-received" condition with an allowance for normal wear and tear.

The Cityrider brand was extended to council-produced publicity and timetables. Council-owned bus stop flags featured an Optare Solo in Cityrider colours.

The Cityrider scheme would see a total of 26 buses, all single-deckers, being purchased new between 2002 and 2009, during an era of generous government spending. These would be operated at various times by D&G Bus, Wardle Transport, Scragg's of Bucknall, Procters of Fenton and First Potteries. Wardle Transport was the only company to have operated every vehicle, though not all at the same time. D&G Bus also operated all of the vehicles, apart from the three Optare Aleros. At the other

extreme, Scragg's had one Versa and a couple of Solos, First Potteries only operated one Dart and one Versa, and Procters only ever operated a single Solo.

From 2010 onwards, however, central government spending cuts would start biting into council spending, which would in turn mean the end of buying new buses and ultimately subsidising socially-necessary bus services. This in turn would lead to the decline of Cityrider, and the subsequent sale of most of the vehicles to raise much-needed cash to help plug gaps in council spending elsewhere. By April 2016 just eight buses, four Solos and four Versas, would be owned by the council out of the original 26.

The first vehicles arrived in February 2002 when three 51-registered Dennis Dart SLFs with Alexander 29-seat bodywork were delivered wearing the Cityrider red, white and blue livery and were

LEFT: **Wardle Transport SlimLine Solo BU54 ALL was delivered new in Cityrider livery as shown on page 25, but is seen here after a repaint into Wardle's red and white.**

BELOW LEFT: **The first Cityrider vehicle operated by First Potteries was Dennis Dart DA51 XTD seen here at Chell Heath on its regular route, the 76 between Chell Heath, Tunstall and Middleport. in May 2009.**

with an appropriate DG52 registration. These would be the last Dennises to be purchased by Cityrider. All future deliveries would be sourced from Optare.

Three 12-seat Optare Alero minibuses were purchased in October 2002 and allocated to Wardle Transport, a newcomer to operating service buses in Stoke-on-Trent, for new services 898 and 899 linking Norton, Bradeley Village and Haywood Hospital, which included a demand-responsive section that had to be booked in advance. This allowed the bus to deviate off route to pick up elderly or disabled passengers and take them to the doctors' surgery or to a hospital appointment. The Aleros were in Cityrider livery but also had a light grey skirt and carried Cityrider On Call fleetnames to reflect the demand-responsive nature of the route. They had the appearance more of a stretched limousine than a bus.

allocated to the D&G Bus fleet. At that time D&G Bus operated solely tendered services with second-hand Mercedes minibuses, so this was to be quite a culture change for the staff and passengers. A further four similar vehicles arrived in September 2002, again being allocated to the D&G fleet and put to work on the D&G tendered network, interestingly this time

BELOW: **This Cityrider Optare Versa was delivered new to Wardle Transport in its red and white livery with select registration WT08 BUS. It is seen here when new in May 2011 on route 62 at Ball Green, carrying Arriva fleetnumber 2961.**

More Optare vehicles arrived in September 2003 when the first five Solos were delivered. These 53-registered 27 seaters were again allocated to D&G. They were followed by further Solos but this time the new SlimLine version. Three 23-seaters with 54 registrations arrived in December 2004, with another three 27-seaters, now 05-registered, following in March 2005. These were allocated again to D&G, which by now was operating 18 Cityrider vehicles on its plethora of subsidised bus routes. Wardle Transport received a 23-seater SlimLine Solo which received cherished registration BU54 ALL (Bus for all). This was allocated to route 898 which was proving so popular that the Optare Aleros were having capacity problems.

In 2006 the four DG52-registered Dennis Darts were transferred from D&G Bus to the steadily expanding Wardle Transport operation at Burslem. Surprisingly they were repainted into Wardle's red and white livery for new routes 62/62A from Hanley to Burslem via Ball Green and Haywood Hospital. The Hanley to Ball Green section was a replacement for First Potteries route 42 which had been recently withdrawn without replacement, the remainder of the route replaced the Optare Aleros on the 898. The demand-responsive element of the 898 was poorly used and was subsequently withdrawn. The 62/62A were partly subsidised and partly commercial. Two of the earlier 51-registered Darts were also transferred from D&G to Wardle and repainted red and white. The Optare Aleros were then sold.

As Wardle continued to win more council tenders, mainly at the expense of D&G, so it continued to receive more council buses, this time more Optare Solos. Some of these Solos also received Wardle Transport livery.

Up to this point all vehicles had been delivered new in Cityrider livery, but this was to change in 2008 with the delivery of three 38-seat Optare Versas with cherished registrations for Wardle Transport. WT08 BUS and WT58 BUS were delivered in Wardle Transport red and white livery. WT58 BUS had been allocated YJ58 PHK at Optare before the cherished

ABOVE: **When First Potteries received this Optare Versa in November 2009 it was the first Versa in the First Group fleet. It was numbered 49001 and is seen at Stanfields on service 76 a week before the route was withdrawn in May 2011.**

registration was chosen.

The third Optare Versa, WT58 SOT (for Stoke-on-Tent), arrived in a new dark purple and silver livery with leather seats, laminate floors and polished wheeltrims for the new Plumline service linking Hanley and Blurton via the Trentham Lakes business park. Although commissioned by the council, the Plumline and associated workers' route 500 from Norton to Trentham Lakes were funded by St Modwen, the developer of the Trentham Lakes complex situated on the site of the former Hem Heath colliery. Developer contributions were obtained by the council as part of the planning

RIGHT: **Wardle Transport Optare Versa WT58 SOT, in the original Plumline livery of dark maroon and silver, is seen in Hanley in June 2011 with Arriva fleet number 2963.**

BELOW RIGHT: **The first Cityrider vehicle for Scragg's was this Optare Solo which previously carried Wardle's red livery and was repainted white with Scragg's Blue Buses fleetnames. It is seen here at the old Hanley Bus Station in July 2011.**

ABOVE: **Short Optare Versa YJ59 GHH is seen working with D&G Bus in Hanley on route 85 to Crewe in March 2014, taking a Cityrider vehicle well out of the Stoke-on-Trent area.**

process for large developments. The aim was to provide bus services for employees of companies reallocating to Trentham Lakes.

The two bus-seated Versas provided extra capacity on routes 62/62A, and also acted as spares for the Plumline service. Wardle was allowed to paint the buses in its own livery, on condition that if they were ever transferred to another operator they would pay to have them repainted into Cityrider livery or into a livery agreeable to that operator.

In spring 2009 First Potteries received its first Cityrider vehicle, one of the 51-registered Dennis

Darts which was transferred from D&G when First won route 76, Chell Heath to Middleport via Tunstall. This was only a temporary allocation pending delivery of the final Cityrider vehicle, a 34-seat Optare Versa. It joined First Potteries in November 2009 in Cityrider colours as its 49001, with branding for the 76. It was the first Versa to be operated by any FirstGroup subsidiary and was allocated to Adderley Green garage.

Scragg's of Bucknall acquired one of the 2004 Optare Solo SlimLines which was repainted from Wardle Transport red and white to all over white with Blue Buses fleetnames. It didn't stay too long at Scragg's, soon returning to Wardle but this time staying white with Wardle fleetnames. Procters of Fenton received its one and only Cityrider-liveried Optare Solo, YN53 EMJ, for tendered route 70, Bentilee to Stoke. The Solo also occasionally appeared at Leek on service 16 from Hanley. It received Procters fleetnames on Cityrider livery.

From May 2011 council subsidies for bus services - which in 2010 amounted to £347,000, including

LEFT: **Procters only ever operated one Cityrider vehicle, Optare Solo YN53 EMJ, officially allocated for route 70, Bentilee to Stoke. It suffered engine failure before Procters closed down in March 2013, but by then route 70 had already been withdrawn. It was towed to Arriva's Adderley Green garage for storage. It is seen here at awaiting disposal in August 2015, two and a half years later.**

£33,900 developer contributions - were drastically cut, making the future for unremunerative bus services look increasingly bleak. As services were withdrawn due to the reduction in funds, Cityrider buses became increasingly redundant. Put simply, the bus services that they were originally purchased for were rapidly disappearing.

First Potteries lost its Optare Versa following the cancellation of route 76 by the council at the end of May 2011. It was transferred to Wardle Transport for a shorter version of the route. This was to be the last Cityrider bus operated by First Potteries.

Following the purchase by Arriva Midlands of Wardle Transport in 2010 and the D&G depot at Longton, Stoke-on-Trent in 2011, the Wardle depot in Burslem was closed and all vehicles gradually relocated to the Longton depot of D&G. The enlarged operation, now known as Arriva Wardle Transport, found itself operating the majority of the Cityrider buses. These gradually started to be parked up, with Arriva preferring to use surplus buses from other Arriva Midlands depots.

In March 2012 Stoke-on-Trent City Council announced that it was looking to sell eight surplus Darts and Solos for £80,000. They also suggested that they might raise up to £650,000 if they sold all the Cityrider buses for their book value, but

if it did this it would have to repay the developer contribution money. Selling all the buses could see even more socially necessary services disappear as operators would not be prepared to buy buses to operate marginally profitable routes. It also discussed leasing out the buses, but as some were now over ten years old the returns would be relatively low. Eventually it was agreed to tender services with a nil financial content, but with a bus provided; but the majority of the oldest buses that were now surplus to requirements would be sold.

When Procters suddenly closed down in March 2013, and before all the assets were sold off by auction, its Cityrider Optare Solo, which had previously suffered engine failure and was a non-runner, was towed to the Arriva Wardle Transport garage at Longton for further storage, joining around 15 other surplus Cityrider Darts and Solos already stored there. Most of these buses were parked up for over two years in the open, exposed to the elements and gradually deteriorating, with the council incurring a monthly storage charge by Arriva.

In January 2014 the D&G Bus depot at Crewe, which had not been purchased by Arriva in 2011, was successful in winning the Plumline and associated service 500 contract from Arriva Wardle Transport. It was to be doubled in frequency so the four Cityrider Optare Versas were transferred to Crewe. D&G also agreed to divert its service 85, Crewe to Hanley via Penkhull, on Sundays to replace a withdrawn subsidised route using one of these Versas. WT08 BUS and WY58 SOT in Wardle livery and old Plumline livery were repainted into a new dark cream, white and purple Plumline livery. WT58 BUS received its first coat of Cityrider red, white and blue. Original plans by the council to refurbish one of the bus-seated Versas to match WT58 SOT with leather seats and laminate floors were quietly

dropped. As spare buses, the two Cityrider-liveried Versas often appeared on other D&G routes, like the 85 from Crewe to Newcastle, as well as on Crewe town services on weekdays, giving the prospect of Cityrider buses operating well outside the Stoke-on-Trent city boundary.

After many false starts the council finally started selling the surplus Cityrider buses in spring 2015 via an online auction, with successful bidders soon removing them from the Wardle Transport yard. The sale by Arriva of Wardle Transport back to D&G Bus in May 2015 saw the Plumline route and the three Versas that were operating it at Crewe transferring back to Potteries. The Plumline route and service 500 were both withdrawn in 2015, being incorporated into new D&G routes 14 and 14A, Norton – Hanley – Stafford, but continuing to provide a service via Trentham Lakes as it received developer contribution funding. The fourth Versa, YJ59 GHH, had since been transferred to Scragg's who were operating it on route 50 Hanley to Caverswell via Longton, one of the few subsidised services left.

As at April 2016, only eight buses remained in

BELOW: **One of four Cityrider Optare Solos still owned by the council, YJ54 BSY has been repainted in Scragg's attractive blue livery and is seen at Abbey Hulton in February 2016.**

council ownership. There were the four Versas, three with D&G and one with Scragg's, and the four 2004 SlimLine Solos, running with Scragg's on three "nil financial support" contracts. These were route 90, Tunstall to Ball Green, route 44, Hanley to Stanley, and the 80 linking Hanley and Eaton Park by way of Bucknall and Bentilee. The 44 receives some subsidy from Staffordshire County Council as it is a cross-boundary service.

Service cuts have seen some areas of Stoke-on-Trent such as Middleport, Bradeley Village and Wedgewood Farm no longer having a bus service on their doorsteps, meaning residents now have to walk up to half a mile to access one. Many estate roads and housing schemes that were once served by buses are now devoid of

them, with little prospect of them returning.

Optare Solo YJ54 BSY is notable in having supported four different liveries in council ownership – Cityrider, Wardle Transport white with Blue Buses and Wardle fleetnames, and Scragg's blue. And Optare Versa YJ59 GHH has worked for four different operators, First Potteries, Wardle Transport, D&G and Scragg's, all while keeping its Cityrider livery.

Scragg's purchased the three 05-registered Solos in the online auction and has painted two into its attractive Blue Buses livery. Some of these have subsequently received cherished registrations. YJ05 JXR is now 1590 VT and YJ05 JXS is 9685 VT, interestingly both original Stoke-on-Trent numbers. ∎

Cityrider bus fleet

Registration	Chassis	Body	New
DA51 XTC	Dennis Dart SLF	Alexander B29F	2/2002
DA51 XTD	Dennis Dart SLF	Alexander B29F	2/2002
DA51 XTE	Dennis Dart SLF	Alexander B29F	2/2002
DG52 TYP	Dennis Dart SLF	Alexander B29F	9/2002
DG52 TYS	Dennis Dart SLF	Alexander B29F	9/2002
DG52 TYT	Dennis Dart SLF	Alexander B29F	9/2002
DG52 TYU	Dennis Dart SLF	Alexander B29F	9/2002
YP52 BPE	Optare Alero	B12F	10/2002
YP52 BPF	Optare Alero	B12F	10/2002
YP52 BPK	Optare Alero	B12F	10/2002
YN53 EMF	Optare Solo	B27F	10/2003
YN53 EMJ	Optare Solo	B27F	10/2003
YN53 EMK	Optare Solo	B27F	10/2003
YN53 EMV	Optare Solo	B27F	10/2003
YN53 EMX	Optare Solo	B27F	10/2003
BU54 ALL	Optare Solo SlimLine	B23F	12/2004
YJ54 BSX	Optare Solo SlimLine	B23F	12/2004
YJ54 BSY	Optare Solo SlimLine	B23F	12/2004
YJ54 BSZ	Optare Solo SlimLine	B23F	12/2004
YJ05 JXP	Optare Solo SlimLine	B27F	3/2005
YJ05 JXR	Optare Solo SlimLine	B27F	3/2005
YJ05 JXS	Optare Solo SlimLine	B27F	3/2005
WT08 BUS	Optare Versa	B38F	4/2008
WT58 BUS	Optare Versa	B38F	11/2008
WT58 SOT	Optare Versa	DP38F	11/2008
YJ59 GHH	Optare Versa	B34F	11/2009

Five decades of change on the Fylde

Mark Bailey reviews bus operations in one of Britain's busiest coastal areas.

ABOVE: **At the start of the 1970s Lytham St Annes Corporation was still running four all-Leyland PD1s dating from 1946. This bus was withdrawn in 1972 and is now preserved by the Lancastrian Transport Trust. It is pictured in September 2011 having just left the LTT depot at Marton for Blackpool town centre on a free service linking participating Heritage Open Day sites.**

The Fylde peninsula in Lancashire is bounded by the Irish Sea to the west, the Ribble estuary to the south and Morecambe Bay to the north. There is no definitive eastern boundary but it roughly follows the line of the A6. The main centre of population is Blackpool, with Lytham St Annes, Fleetwood, Thornton Cleveleys, Poulton-le-Fylde and Kirkham other urban areas of significance.

At the start of the 1970s local transport was provided by two municipal operators - Blackpool Corporation and Lytham St Annes Corporation - and by National Bus Company subsidiary Ribble Motor Services. Local government changes in 1974 saw the Lytham St Annes authority replaced by Fylde Borough Council. The 1985 Transport Act forced local authorities to divest themselves of direct bus operation and thus in October 1986 Blackpool Transport Services Ltd and Fylde Borough Transport Ltd were formed. In December 1993 the Fylde undertaking was bought by its management team as Fylde Transport Ltd, only to be sold on in May 1994 to Blackpool, effectively returning the business from the private sector back into municipal control. It was initially kept separate but was fully absorbed in July 1996. The former Lytham St Annes Corporation depot at Squires Gate was closed in 1999 and demolished a couple of years later.

A further consequence of the 1985 Transport Act was the break-up of the National Bus Company and in April 1989 Ribble became part of the growing Stagecoach empire. In Blackpool, Ribble's large depot at Devonshire Road was closed and demolished in 1987, followed by the closure of its Talbot Road depot in 1988. The town's gloomy Talbot Road bus station, situated beneath a multi-storey car park, ceased to be used in 2002, with buses using neighbouring streets instead.

In the 1970s Blackpool was still a popular destination for holidays and day trips, particularly for families in the industrial towns of northern England and Scotland when mills and factories closed down for a week or two, known as wakes weeks. On summer Saturdays or Illuminations weekends several thousand coaches and buses would arrive in the town on a network of express services and excursions. The Coliseum coach station was the main hub of activity, with vehicles often queued nose to tail along Lytham Road awaiting entry. Many of these were working the X60 service from Manchester, where fully-laden double-deckers would arrive every few minutes. Yelloway Motor Services had its own coach station on Bloomfield Road, used also by Premier Travel, Barton Transport and others.

Blackpool coach operator WC Standerwick, a subsidiary of Ribble since the 1930s, ceased to exist in April 1974 when it was assimilated into newly-formed National Travel (North West). Coaches were repainted all-over white and the Standerwick name, albeit in small lettering, lived on for a few more years.

Today Blackpool Transport is by far the dominant operator in the area, and remains one of only 11 surviving municipally-owned operators in Britain. A £100million project to rebuild the 11-mile tramway infrastructure and update the rolling stock was completed in 2012, and included a new depot at Starr Gate and sixteen Bombardier Flexity 2 trams. There are plans to extend the line from Talbot Square to Blackpool North railway station, restoring a link that was withdrawn in 1963. Investment in high-quality new buses saw the arrival of ten Euro6-engined Mercedes-Benz Citaros in 2015, with ten Alexander Dennis Enviro400 City double-deckers following in 2016.

April 2016 saw retrenchment by Stagecoach with the closure of Fleetwood depot - its last on the Fylde - and cessation of all local services, but Stagecoach still works into Blackpool from Preston and Lancaster. Coastal Coaches provides essential rural connections with a modern fleet, and Catch22Bus has expanded to plug gaps in the Blackpool Transport network and to serve areas where Stagecoach has pulled out. ∎

BELOW: **Blackpool Corporation continued to take delivery of traditional front-engined double-deckers until 1968, one of the last operators to do so. The Leyland Titan had been the chassis of choice since the early 1930s, with the majority having full front bodywork. The final batches were bodied by Metro-Cammell to half-cab specification, as illustrated by this line up of preserved Titan PD3As at the Rigby Road depot open day in September 2010.**

TOP: **Much of the tramway rolling stock at the dawn of the 1970s was already 35 years old, and today some remain operational in the heritage fleet having amassed over 80 years of service. Open Boat 604 and Balloon 717 were both still in regular service when photographed in September 2010 during the tramway's 125th anniversary year.**

MIDDLE: **Ribble had provided a comprehensive network of services in and around Fleetwood since the early 1930s. In the 1970s these were operated by a mixture of Leyland Leopards, Leyland Nationals and Bristol REs. Illustrating the last of these types is 229, seen working the F10 in Thornton Cleveleys in May 1978. Sadly the Fleetwood depot closed in April 2016 following the withdrawal of bus subsidies by Lancashire County Council.**

BOTTOM: **The first new vehicles delivered to Fylde Borough Council were a pair of Plaxton-bodied Leyland Leopard PSU3B/4R coaches in 1974. One is pictured in Lytham in May 1979 working service 31A to Blackpool. Fylde vehicles – single- and double-deckers – were often hired on summer Saturdays to Ribble and National Travel to help move the large number of passengers heading to and from Blackpool on their holidays.**

ABOVE: **Since 1930 Abbotts of Blackpool had operated a frequent daily express service linking Fleetwood and north Blackpool with Bolton and Manchester. For many years the fleet was standardised on the AEC Reliance, and a pair of Harrington-bodied examples are pictured at the Cleveleys depot in May 1979. The company later moved into the former Ribble depot on Talbot Road but sadly went into voluntary liquidation in 2000.**

LEFT: **From 1969 to 1974 Blackpool Corporation placed 55 AEC Swifts in service with dual-door bodywork by Marshall of Cambridge. 559 is seen in June 1979 in Grange Park working service 5 to Halfway House.**

RIGHT: **It wasn't until 1977 that Blackpool Corporation took delivery of its first rear-engined double-deckers, nine years after its final Titan PD3s. Leyland Atlanteans with East Lancs bodywork were the favoured combination and the very first, 301, is seen at Bispham in February 1978 working service 22 from Cleveleys to Halfway House.**

BELOW: **Following deregulation Blackpool Transport registered routes in St Annes, prompting retaliation by Fylde Borough Transport, which had rebranded itself as Blue Buses. In 1987 it introduced six new Baby Blues minibuses to target tramway passengers along Blackpool promenade. 104, a Northern Counties-bodied Dodge S56, is pictured at Talbot Square in September 1987 with a full load heading south on service 5 from Gynn Square to the Pontins Holiday Camp. Competition was extended at the end of the holiday season to serve Cleveleys, the success of which led to further minibuses arriving the following year.**

ABOVE: **In 1986 Blackpool Transport acquired six AEC Routemasters from London Buses, with a further six arriving in 1988. They wore a red and white livery and retained RM fleet numbers as a nod to their heritage. 526 (RM 1735) is seen at Squires Gate in September 1987 working the 12 from Blackpool to St Annes.**

ABOVE: **The deregulation of local bus services in October 1986 saw the start of new operators and routes and stimulated competition on existing routes. The first change to the status quo on the Fylde came earlier that year in March, when Mather of Blackpool, trading as Easyway Bus, introduced new service 53 linking Poulton-le-Fylde with Blackpool Airport at Squires Gate, avoiding the town centre. Pictured in September 1986 on the Grange Park estate is NCN 815L, an ex-Northern General Plaxton-bodied Bristol RELH6G.**

ABOVE: **Compared to most of the minibuses that flooded Britain's streets in the mid to late 1980s, Blackpool Transport's were eye-catching Optare CityPacers based on the Volkswagen LT55 chassis. They introduced a new livery of yellow and black, and were branded Handy Bus. Seen in Cleveleys bus station in June 1989 is 576, working service 9 to Blackpool.**

BELOW: **Impressed with Blackpool Transport's new Optare Deltas, Fylde Borough Transport decided to purchase three of its own in 1991. Based on the DAF SB220 chassis, these were attractive and stylish vehicles. The first, with appropriate registration H1 FBT, is photographed a stone's throw from the depot at Squires Gate in August 1992, on service 11 from Cleveleys to Lytham.**

LEFT: **In 1988 Fylde Borough Transport purchased the Blackpool-based business of S&J Wood, better known as Seagull Coaches, along with three vehicles. The acquisition gave Fylde a slice of the day excursion market for holidaymakers, and the Seagull name was retained and applied to other coaches, including a few double-deckers. The sale to Blackpool Transport in 1994 triggered an influx of vehicles from the parent fleet, including East Lancs coach-seated Leyland Atlantean 364. This became Fylde 47 and was repainted into Seagull Coaches livery, as pictured here in August 1995 on a day excursion to Fleetwood.**

RIGHT: **Blackpool Transport relaunched its network in 2001 as Metro Coastlines, with route branding and bold colour schemes applied to the bus fleet and many of the trams. Optare MetroRider 515 illustrates the pink and yellow livery for route 15, seen here arriving in Poulton-le-Fylde from Mereside in September 2008. The Metro Coastlines identity was discontinued in 2010 in favour of a standard yellow and black livery.**

ABOVE: **In recent years the services operated by Stagecoach in and around Fleetwood were provided by Optare Solos, Optare Versas and Alexander Dennis Enviro200s. Pictured when new in September 2008, Ribble 25228 is an Optare Versa seen passing Fleetwood's elegant Queen's Terrace on the 84 to Blackpool via Cleveleys, Thornton and Poulton-le-Fylde. Stagecoach pulled out of Fleetwood in April 2016 following Lancashire County Council subsidy cuts.**

RIGHT: **Coastal Coaches of Warton operates two Fylde Villager services – the 76 and 78 - which link Kirkham and Wesham in rural Fylde with the towns on the coast. Since the withdrawal of subsidies in April 2016 both services have been run commercially. Optare Solo YJ11 EHC is seen when new in April 2011 in Kirkham working Fylde Villager 76, a circuitous route starting in Blackpool and ending in St Annes.**

LEFT: **In September 2012 Classic Bus North West assumed operation of former Blackpool Transport service 22, which ran from Cleveleys to Halfway House; this was then extended to Mereside. Now run under the guise of Catch22Bus, Plaxton-bodied Dennis Dart SLF W466 UAG, new to East Yorkshire and latterly with their Whittles subsidiary in Kidderminster, is pictured in Blackpool in April 2016. The livery of turquoise and orange is based on that of Cardiff Bus. Following the Stagecoach withdrawal the 22 has been extended beyond Cleveleys to serve Fleetwood.**

Following a four-year refurbishment of the tramway infrastructure, which included track replacement and the construction of longer and higher wheelchair-accessible platforms at tram stops, 16 Bombardier Flexity 2 trams were introduced in 2012. These sport a new livery of white and maroon, the latter being the colour of Blackpool Council. Nicknamed by some as the Bond tram, 007 is seen during its first week in service in April 2012 at Fleetwood Ferry. A fleet of heritage trams has been retained for seasonal use.

BELOW: The newest single-deckers in the Blackpool Transport fleet are ten Euro6-engined Mercedes-Benz Citaro O295s delivered in 2015. They have replaced ageing Optare Excels, and wear a new grey and primrose livery with Palladium branding. No. 557 is pictured in April 2016 approaching Blackpool's Victoria Hospital on service 5 from Halfway House.

The heyday of East Kent

Michael Baker takes a fond look back at the operations of the East Kent Road Car Company.

In the introduction to the 1949 edition of Ian Allan's ABC of East Kent Buses and Coaches we read: "The outbreak of war in 1939 wrought havoc with the carefully developed scheme of things in the East Kent area, and in a public statement, the company described the probable effect on the company's fortunes as disastrous."

This was no exaggeration as the Battle of Britain was fought above, the buses of the East Kent Road Car Company were going about their business. In one instance a Canterbury-bound bus was attacked from the air, the conductress noticing "sparks flying from the road" and was about to signal the driver to stop when the bus veered off into a field, the driver

All photographs by the author or from the author's collection.

A 1936 Brush-bodied Leyland Titan TD4 posed for a photograph illustrating East Kent's maintenance procedures, although it is unlikely a bus would have received this type of attention in what appears to be the middle of the garage rather than in the workshop area.

having been killed by a machine-gun bullet.

On another occasion, again near Canterbury, a bomb exploded just behind the bus, killing the conductress and several passengers. The ABC records that, "despite the fact that the German aircraft was still about, another bus, without hesitation, went into the same area to pick up the passengers". The area round Dover, well within range of Nazi guns mounted on the French coast, became known as "the unhealthiest health resort in England". East Kent prepared special signs which, when the shelling grew excessive – one would like to know how they measured excessive – were placed upon bus stops reading "Shelling Warning in Operation, Services Nos 90-92 depart from 'The Engineer' Folkestone Road."

My very first visit to East Kent territory was a year before the outbreak of war, to Broadstairs, by coach, or charabanc as older members of the family still liked to call motor coaches, from our home in Croydon, although it would not have been in an East Kent vehicle, more likely one operated by Bourne and Balmer or John Bennett.

My next visit was in 1947, dad and I spending a weekend in Hythe and Folkestone. I was impressed by the deep red livery of the buses which plied a frequent service along the edge of the sea through Sandgate to Folkestone, interspersed from time to time by tall dark green and off white Leyland Titans of Maidstone & District, which jointly worked the 36-mile-long route 10, all the way from Maidstone. The height of these Titans struck me on account of

ABOVE: **East Kent's buses were smartly turned-out, as shown by another TD4 on the 36-mile-long route 10 from Folkestone to Maidstone. The badge on the radiator reads "East Kent", rather than "Leyland".**

practically all East Kent double-deckers being of lowbridge specification, even working routes, like the 10, where highbridge ones were permitted.

Sandgate has always been a favourite place of mine, lying just beyond Folkestone's Leas where set on the cliff tops is some of the finest seaside architecture in England. Sandgate itself is not without architectural distinction but its chief attraction is that on a clear

ABOVE: **Canterbury Bus Station in wartime, with two Leyland Titans and a Dennis Lance. The Titan on the left is in wartime red and grey livery. A sign above the booking office on the left describes the premises rather grandly as "St Peter's Road Car Station".**

Curiously five TS1 Tigers, a chassis designed as a single-decker, were bought in 1928-29 and fitted with double-deck open-top Short bodies. Equally unusual was the shine East Kent took, almost uniquely, to Morris Commercial products. In fact Edinburgh Corporation was the only other purchaser of the Morris Commercial Imperial double-decker. East Kent had 30 in all, entering the fleet in 1932-33. They could not have been a very satisfactory purchase for all were withdrawn in 1939 leaving the older Leylands to soldier on, mostly to the end of the war, although I have no recollection of seeing any of them. Much more appreciated than the Morris Commercials were five Daimler COG5s with highbridge Weymann bodies which had belonged to the Isle of Thanet Tramways. Dating from 1936 – the trams disappeared a year later - they lasted until 1950.

Contemporary with the Titans was a fleet of TS7 and TS8 Tiger coaches. Again the parallels with Maidstone & District and Southdown were there for all to see for each had a fleet of Tigers with handsome, indeed luxurious bodies by a variety of builders, Harrington, Beadle and Park Royal chiefly, but all very similar. Of East Kent's Park Royal-bodied Tigers 24 were converted to ambulances during the war, whilst a further 62 travelled all over the United Kingdom carrying entertainers belong to ENSA, the Entertainments National Service Association. Those of a cynical bent used to claim that the initials stood for 'Every Night Something Awful' which was a bit unfair for although the quality of entertainment offered the troops and the factory workers – remember Worker's Playtime broadcast on the BBC Home Service? - did vary considerably, at the top end were such stars as Arthur Askey, Gracie Fields, George Formby and Laurence Olivier. Not

day it is perfectly possible to see the French coast, whilst clear or not, there are always ships proceeding up and down the Channel, often these days huge container ones, although back in 1946 there would have been many more small coasters, and a great variety of freighters, many, like their crews, survivors of the war. Then there was and is a constant procession of buses, the upper deck being a perfect grandstand for views out to sea.

Leylands dominated the East Kent fleet, or rather two thirds of it, in 1947. This I considered only right and proper as they also dominated the Southdown and, to an extent, the Maidstone & District fleets. Between them the three companies had a virtual monopoly of the south-eastern counties of Kent and Sussex whereas the AEC was the standard for my home London Transport fleet. There were, of course, exceptions to this rule but nevertheless it seemed to me a neat division.

The Leyland Titan had been the standard East Kent double-decker of the later 1930s. Twenty TD4s with 53-seat Brush bodies arrived in 1936, followed by 50 more with very similar Park Royal bodies in 1936-37. In 1938 another 41 were put into service, this time TD5s, 28 with Park Royal, 13 with Brush bodies but all to East Kent specifications. Finally in 1939 another 28 Park Royal-bodied TD5s arrived. The first Titans, six TD1s with Leyland bodies, entered the fleet in 1930, with four more following in 1931.

TOP: **Early post-war purchases included 50 Leyland Titans with Leyland bodywork. This, the last, was a PD2; the remainder were PD1s.**

MIDDLE: **After the Titans East Kent switched to Guy Arabs with Park Royal bodies. The first had bodies of a style broadly similar to that fitted to London Transport's RT-class Regents and RTL-class Titans.**

BOTTOM: **Coach-air services featured in East Kent's operations from the 1950s. This 1951 Royal Tiger is ready to run from London to Lympne Airport from where passengers will fly by Silver City Airways to Beauvais and then catch another coach to Paris.**

all the coaches returned to peace time service with the company but by the end of 1947 delivery of 50 PS1 Tigers with the inevitable Park Royal bodywork, similar to the pre-war coaches but slightly modernised, had covered wartime losses so that no coaches dated back beyond 1935.

We have noted that some two-thirds of the fleet were Leylands. The other third, approximately, was made up of Dennis Lancets. Tilling-Stevens, a Maidstone based firm, had been enormously popular in south-eastern England, and until 1936 the East Kent single-deck bus fleet had comprised nothing else. But Tilling-Stevens had not kept up with the huge strides made by AEC and Leyland in the late 1920s and early 1930s, nor indeed with other manufacturers, and in 1934 the first of 20 Dennis Aces were bought by East Kent. But this was merely a prelude to a huge influx of the larger Dennis Lancets which entered the single-deck fleet between 1936 and 1949. The first 25 had a rather clumsy radiator but the rest, including the post-war ones, sported the much more elegantly curved top and bottom version which became so familiar all over Kent and Sussex. Many of the pre-war ones with Dennis bodies were rebodied after the war by Park Royal with bodies virtually identical to those fitted to the post-war Lancets.

In the early days of the second world war East Kent found that, with the complete absence of holidaymakers, it could lend vehicles to other, hard-pressed companies, but as the war continued the combination of war work and severe restrictions on private motoring meant that new buses were needed and so the Guy Arab entered the fleet. Highbridge as well as lowbridge examples arrived. Like other bus companies East Kent was not much impressed by the quality of the bodies but it liked the Arab chassis and after the war it added 125 between 1950 and 1957, all with Park Royal bodies. By this time a number of low railway bridges head

either been raised or abandoned and all East Kent double-deckers new from 1951 were of highbridge layout, which considerably reduced the incidence of headaches amongst the company's passengers.

The company's early Arabs had exposed radiators, the later ones concealed tin fronts. Some of both varieties had bodies which followed closely the style of the London RT: Park Royal, of course, built several

thousand of these. London Transport had thoughts about putting the RT body on the Arab and did buy one Arab chassis but with provincial style bodywork and then dropped the idea. So the nearest we could have got to what the a Guy version of the RT (RTG?) would have looked like is the 1951 FFN-series of East Kent Guys. Incidentally East Kent did not get around to numbering its fleet until 1977, making do with registrations along until then.

East Kent stayed faithful to Dennis at the beginning of the underfloor era, ordering in 1954 30 Lancet UFs with handsome Duple Ambassador lV coach bodies, following on from six Leyland Royal Tigers with rather fussy Park Royal bodies and two with Duple Coronation Ambassador bodies, not unlike those fitted to the UF Lancets. My first view of an underfloor Lancet was at London's Victoria Coach Station. I was much impressed, not least by plenty of chromium moulding which might have been thought excessive, but not by me. Sadly the Lancets were not particularly successful and, indeed, ended East Kent's long association with the make. Even Aldershot & District, the most enthusiastic supporter of Dennis (which, seeing their factory was in A&D territory at Guildford, was not surprising), gave up on the underfloor Lancet and instead opted for the

AEC Reliance, which was exactly what East Kent did.

However before that East Kent went off in a rather unusual direction coach-wise. Inevitably after the years of wartime neglect, the bodywork on its Titans was in a very poor state. Many were fitted with new Park Royal or, rather unusually, ECW lowbridge bodies, but most of the final AJG-registered ones had their chassis modified and were given Beadle coach bodies. Beadle was a local firm, more or less, its factory being in Dartford, and Maidstone & District and Southdown went down the same route, and for a couple of years a visit to Victoria Coach Station would find practically every coach headed for the Medway Towns and the Kent Coast being a Beadle. Only on summer weekends would the older half-cabs put in an appearance. The Beadle rebuilds were an interesting, cost-cutting attempt to convince passengers that these were modern vehicles, comparable to underfloor-engined ones and quite handsome. Presumably Maidstone & District passengers were not taken in for their Beadles were soon relegated to bus work but East Kent's were still on excursion and long-distance work in the mid 1960s. Two have been preserved. They were certainly more modern looking than the 25 Lancets which were delivered in 1950, their Park Royal coach bodies looking like something which might have been built 15 years earlier. They were relegated to bus work, for which they were singularly unsuited.

In 1955 East Kent, like so many other companies, found that the AEC Reliance was exactly what it had been looking for. The 40 delivered in that year had neat Weymann bodies and were intended for both bus and coach work. Truth to tell they looked rather more like buses than coaches, as did a further batch, this time with Beadle bodywork which had echoes of the Leyland/Beadle rebuilds. In 1960 Park Royal found itself back in favour with some rather nice, if not particularly grand looking 41-seat dual-purpose vehicles and the company had obviously decided that pure coaches were neither needed nor a selling point with passengers. The previous year 25 post-war Lancets were rebuilt as forward-entrance one-man-operated buses, another form of compromise which did not exactly result in a thing of beauty. I can recall being conveyed from Dover Priory station down to the docks in one, a reminder of the Elvis Presley classic "Shake, rattle and roll".

The first 36-footers arrived in 1962. These were proper coaches, Reliances with 46-seat Park Royal bodies and were the first of many. Later, in 1964-65 came a variation with big windows, which improved an already well-proportioned vehicle. The 36-foot long BET style of single-deck bus, a nice design with a number of variations but a strong family likeness, first entered the fleet in 1965. Very similar vehicles appeared in considerable numbers in the Maidstone & District and Southdown fleets; indeed 30 Southdown Leopards with this style of bodywork were transferred to East Kent in 1971. By then the National Bus Company had been formed, and it seemed very likely that East Kent and Maidstone & District would merge.

But that is beyond our brief and we will draw the story of the coach and single-deck East Kent fleet to a close and move on to the contemporary double-deckers. Here again AEC was in favour which was rather odd on two counts. Firstly, although the Reliance was an obvious choice the company had never owned an AEC double-decker and secondly, as early as 1959 Maidstone & District had invested heavily in the rear-engined Leyland Atlantean and many other companies were edging away from the front-engined, half-cab double-decker.

East Kent invested in 1959 in 40 AEC Regent Vs with Park Royal 72-seat forward-entrance bodies. These were splendid-looking vehicles, some of the most handsome double-deckers ever to wear East Kent livery. Then in 1961, a period when, led by the horrible MCW Orion, double-deck bus designers seemed intent on providing as little comfort as possible inside and abandoned the notion of a well-proportioned outside, Park Royal foisted upon East

Kent a batch of truly ugly, half-cab, forward-entrance, sparsely-furnished Regents. Both Park Royal and AEC were clearly losing their way.

In the meantime more Regents joined the fleet, the last in 1967. It would be two years before any more double-deckers arrived. Finally East Kent, with production of the Regent coming to an end, decided that it would join the modern world and in 1969 twenty Daimler Fleetlines took up work. These, as always, had Park Royal bodies but what a difference to those on the later Regents. There was something reminiscent of the first full-front Regents of ten years earlier about them and the handsome East Kent livery displayed their excellent proportions to advantage. This was the very last flowering of the traditional deep red and cream livery for no more double-deckers would join the fleet until 1976 by which time dull National red had taken over, a change which did nothing for any of the vehicles to which it was applied.

Fortunately the preservationists have ensured that the traditional dark red and cream lives on and can be seen out and about all over Kent and beyond. ■

TOP: **The first rear-engined double-deckers for the fleet were 20 Daimler Fleetlines in 1969, also bodied by Park Royal. These were the last double-deckers to be delivered in the company's traditional colours. RFN 953G is preserved.**

BOTTOM: **Preserved buses ensure that the heyday of East Kent Road Car Company is not forgotten. This is a 1937 Leyland Tiger TS8 with Park Royal bodywork.**

Four Friends in an Ami 8

Tony Greaves remembers ambitious weekend bus safaris.

I met Richard in early 1973 at a transport enthusiasts' meeting. During the evening's conversation he suggested photographic trips on which all were welcome in his recently-acquired new car, a Citroën Ami 8, conspicuous by virtue of its quirkily stylish bodywork. It was supremely comfortable, as were all Citroëns of the period, and ideal for long-distance cruising. We were always amused that its air-cooled 602cc engine could propel it to speeds of 80mph - on the flat and downhill - but it slowed to 50 on uphill slopes, all with a full load. We once overtook a Mini 1275GT several times on a late-night journey, with it resuming its position every time we came to a hill. To our surprise we were approached at our next service stop by the driver of the1275GT who asked what we had under the bonnet because he couldn't understand why he couldn't leave us. Imagine his consternation to be told it was less than half the size of his engine and we had a full load compared with

RIGHT: **A standard ECW-bodied Bristol RELL of Brighton Hove & District, with a centre exit and corporate NBC Southdown fleetname.**

ABOVE: **A Southdown Leyland PD3 in traditional livery but with National Bus Company fleetnames. Some NBC subsidiaries were in great haste to change these, while other companies were very slow, taking months, as if begrudgingly, to acknowledge the new identity. Unfortunately for us, Southdown was one of the former.**

his sole occupancy.

John and I were regular passengers, while Tim, David and Malcolm took turns for the fourth seat when they were available. Sadly, John and David are no longer with us. A Sunday was the usual chosen

RIGHT: **This Eastbourne Corporation Leyland Panther Cub had started life in 1966 as a Leyland Motors demonstrator. It had a Strachans body. The bright orange lettering on the waistband, advertising Travelcards, was an unusual style of marketing for a conservative 1970s municipal operator.**

BELOW RIGHT: **Fifteen almost-new AEC Swifts came to London Country from South Wales Transport in 1971. Three had Willowbrook dual-door bodies and the remainder had Marshall fixed window bodies which later gained sliding ventilators. The Marshalls, based at St Albans, happily retained the attractive LCBS Lincoln green and yellow livery for most of their lives. South Wales red can be seen showing through on the wheels.**

day, especially the one in a long weekend, as Richard was a bus driver and this allowed his recovery before taking up a morning duty.

The original trips were prompted by the recent introduction of National Bus Company corporate liveries, with the object being to photograph the classic liveries before they disappeared for ever, plus any oddball combinations and liveries which in some cases displayed rebellion by the operator. There was an upsurge in the trips in the mid 1970s with the change in status of many municipal operators, some of which involved a change of livery while others just changed the fleetname.

The concept of a day trip was taken to extremes,

BELOW: **London Country Routemaster RCL 2226 sparkles in the sun following a spring shower at Godstone with our transport conveniently parked behind it.**

BELOW RIGHT: **We ended the London Country day with a look at the Superbus experiment at Stevenage. We were keen on Metro-Scania buses, for different reasons – I particularly liked the low proportions of the body inherited from the Swedish CR76 and the bold livery. Richard was impressed by the two-stage transmission, probably more so than the company management. Here Superbus MS1 awaits an evening departure on the Chells service.**

with most days starting with an 0400 pick-up and, for example one trip that included Brighton, Hove and Eastbourne meant a home arrival of after 0200. The motorway network was still being built, so, for example, if we went west from our Leeds base we had to go beyond Huddersfield to pick up the M62. But on a more positive note, Sundays were very quiet on the motorways in the days before the relaxation of Sunday trading laws.

One very memorable trip was to cover as many south coast operators as possible, including Southdown, Brighton Hove & District, which included some recently-transferred Lodekkas curiously wearing Southdown-BH&D fleetnames and Eastbourne.

LEFT: **Southampton Corporation 385 was one of a batch of 20 East Lancashire-bodied AEC Regent Vs supplied in 1966-67, eight of which were finished at East Lancs' Neepsend Coachworks business in Sheffield.**

BELOW LEFT: **Our visit to King Alfred Motor Services in Winchester was unfortunately the day after the company was taken over by Hants & Dorset. The last of the three King Alfred Metro-Scanias had been renumbered into Hants & Dorset's series and had NBC-style grey legal lettering. A few months after this photo was taken all three were transferred to the London Country Superbus fleet.**

depot foreman's office and ask for permission to take photographs. We were nearly always warned about the dangers of falling down pits but we were very rarely refused... and I don't think reflective yellow jackets had been invented. At the time, I felt a little disappointed that we had to resort to so many depot photographs but they have become more interesting with the passage of time and the closure and sale of so many garages, ex-tram sheds and depots.

Often we would be given trophies such as bus stop plates from the scrap pile as a result of merely hinting that we collected such things. The added weight of these, together with the camera gear in the Ami's boot would reverse the car's usual 'nose down' attitude and make the uphill drags even slower.

A goal of visiting every London Country garage was achieved in one day and would have been far easier had the M25 been complete; but we took advantage of the parts that had been opened.

Apart from an idea of what we wanted to cover the days were ad-lib and usually included unscheduled depot visits because the most interesting buses would not be out on service. We would turn up at the

BELOW: **Our visit to Cardiff City Transport's garage revealed three experimental liveries applied to older Guy Arab buses and two of the three are visible in this line-up. In the distance is the already delicensed turquoise bus, on the right is the dark orange bus, while the third was a similar bus in light orange – the livery selected. The AEC Regents are in the previous standard maroon and cream.**

ABOVE: **As a result of local government re-organisation in 1974 the three municipal operators in the Rhymney Valley were merged to form a new operator of that name. A short while before the merger Gelligaer Urban District Council had adopted a new livery based on the colours of the Welsh flag, as seen on this AEC Reliance with Longwell Green body. The preserved Cardiff trolleybus in the background was stored in the open at the Hengoed depot for some time.**

ABOVE: **Caerphilly Urban District Council's 51, a Leyland Tiger PS2 with a Massey body, had been by the time of our visit demoted to driver training. It is now preserved in full Caerphilly UDC livery. Caerphilly was the largest of the three Rhymney Valley constituents.**

Usually, on the return trip in the early hours when the rear seat occupants were asleep, Richard and I got involved in deep conversation with speculation on the future of the bus industry, mainly in order to keep him alert. Topics discussed at great length that I recall were the eventual inevitable break-up of NBC and the Passenger Transport Executives and, on the engineering side, (we would have been laughed at by industry professionals, remembering that I was a graphic artist and Richard a bus driver), electric buses that could have their tiny motors fitted anywhere on the vehicle, even within the wheel hubs, which would dispense with both the rear axle and differential, assuming there would be huge leaps in future battery technology. Little did we know...

The one exception to the single day trip was a weekend trek round Scotland chasing, among other things, the ex Leeds City Transport 'Ring Road OMOs', two batches of dual-door Roe-bodied AEC Reliances, bought by Alexander Greyhound of Arbroath and Aberdeen Corporation respectively. We got them all.

After photographing AA buses on the promenade at Ayr, we returned to the car to find a local resident lurking near the car. Our initial alarm was soon dispelled when the man expressed great interest in the car, to the extent that he lay on his back for a look underneath and after rocking the car to and fro on its suspension, he finished by complimenting Richard on his choice of car.

Happy days. ∎

BELOW: **The seven-strong Bedwas & Machen Urban District Council fleet included this Leyland Titan PD3, new in 1968 with a Massey body which was the last lowbridge body to be built.**

ABOVE: **A Southend Corporation 33ft-long Northern Counties-bodied Daimler Fleetline loads with busy shoppers in failing light on a winter afternoon.**

BELOW: **The Tyne & Wear PTE bought three pre-production Ailsas in 1974, the only ones built with hydraulic braking. Little did I know when I photographed 403 that a few years later I would be driving this and its fellows in my spare time, when they came to Independent Coachways of Horsforth, Leeds.**

ABOVE: **We had decided we must search out A1's Leeds-style Atlantean, an extra bus tagged on the end of a Leeds order, as Roe had customarily done. As with the two other examples, Weardale Motor Services and Colin S Pegg of Caston, the interiors were entirely as Leeds City Transport's own, except for the seat coverings.**

BELOW: **We managed to photograph all seven of the ex Leeds 'Ring Road OMO' AEC Reliances with Roe 41-seat bodies which had been sold to TD Alexander of Arbroath, which traded as Greyhound, and to Aberdeen Corporation. Here the first of the type, 839 CUM. arrives at Alexander's depot.**

An aura of romance

Before the widespread use of colour photography many manufacturers used artists to create eye-catching images for brochures and adverts. **Stewart J Brown** takes a look.

Colour printing used to be expensive. Colour photography used to be expensive too. Which is why the past is so often illustrated in black and white. When this publication first appeared, as *Buses Annual* in 1964, the only colour was on the cover. In the 1940s and 1950s newspapers were illustrated in black and white. Those magazines which did use colour, either editorially or on their advertising pages, used it sparingly.

For companies wishing to draw attention to their products in adverts or in brochures, a low-cost option at that time was what was known as spot colour. This saw the use of a second colour in the printing process which could be used in various ways to add interest. Typically it might be blocks of colour on the page to highlight sections of the text, for headlines, or as a wash over a black-and-white photograph. Some businesses would use spot colour to enhance details of a photograph of a bus, as if representing its livery. The results weren't always very good, as shown on these pages by a 1953 Burlingham advert illustrating a Ribble Seagull in purple.

The use of artists or illustrators was a widespread practice in the publishing business in the early postwar years. They could create idealised settings

4

CROSSLEY
DOUBLE-DECK OMNIBUS

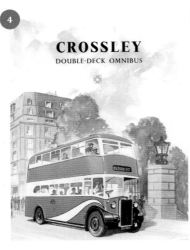

for products, and in particular vehicles. They could also change the proportions of the vehicle, making it look sleeker. This was not unusual among car makers whose illustrators would make dumpy saloons look like elegant limousines. And as will be seen, the same technique was used by coach manufacturers.

Some artists worked from black-and-white photographs to produce coloured images which were distinctly on the rosy side of lifelike. Others added colour to an existing black-and-white photo, a process which can be traced back to Victorian times.

And, as the accompanying images show, some of the coloured illustrations from half a century ago are charming. Some are quaint. And some are just fanciful.

In the immediate postwar period, AEC used spot colour for the heading on the contents page of the *AEC Gazette*, a quarterly magazine of around A5 size which was distributed to the company's customers at home and overseas. The illustration (1) shows a Regal coach, a Regent double-decker and a lorry. It's a whimsical image, and without the spot colour would be nowhere near as attractive.

In September 1946 AEC produced a supplement to the *AEC Gazette* which was devoted to the new Regent III "omnibus chassis". Inside there were coloured illustrations of key mechanical components, but the cover had a picture (2), clearly based on a photograph of a pre-war London Transport RT in Piccadilly Circus. Although the bus was six years old, it was thoroughly modern in appearance thanks to London Transport's high design standards. Many 1940s Regent IIIs would carry considerably less attractive bodywork. The supplement is a work of

art in itself with images which include sectioned drawings of the engine, gearbox and pre-selector transmission control and chassis drawings.

For a lavish postwar brochure which is undated but was probably produced in 1946, Foden also turned to an older vehicle. This coach (3) dated from the mid 1930s and was operated by Staffordshire operator Whieldon's Green Coaches and had striking fully-fronted centre-entrance bodywork. What it didn't have was Foden's distinctive postwar concealed radiator, which has been added by the artist who also added colour to the original black-and-white image. It has been done skilfully – and all long before the advent of Photoshop.

In the brochure Foden notes that "The experience gained from millions of miles of service has been built into our new passenger chassis", but naturally doesn't mention that the picture is of a prewar vehicle. As with AEC's Regent supplement, this brochure contains cut-away images of key components.

Crossley in 1947 issued a brochure with what looks like a Manchester Corporation bus (4), but

9

DAIMLER

Freeline

UNDERFLOOR ENGINE CHASSIS

isn't quite what it seems. The artist appears to have worked from a photograph of a South Shields bus – it has part of a CU-series registration plate and a South Shields-style destination box. And Manchester's postwar buses dispensed with the swooping colour flash on the side. So it's a generic municipal bus with a representation of a crest on the body side. But it's a nice illustration with warm tones.

The October 1948 issue of the *AEC Gazette* highlighted the upcoming Earls Court Commercial Motor Show – the first since 1938 – and featured a coloured drawing of two AECs passing the Earls Court exhibition hall on the cover (5). The Regent has features of the London RT in the livery and the roof route number box, but is an altogether more utilitarian-looking bus with square-cornered windows (on the lower deck only!) and a standard full-height Regent III radiator. The Regent's destination reads "Earls Court" which is

complemented by "Show Special" on the Regal. There's an AEC lorry in the background.

Two years later the world of coaching was changing, with the arrival of a new generation of underfloor-engined vehicles, and with AEC and Leyland taking the lead in terms of sales. In August 1950 Leyland issued a brochure for its new Royal Tiger with a nice illustration of a coach on the front (6). It is shown from an unusually low angle with passengers milling around. Rectangular headlamps are a novel touch. Leyland had to use a hand-drawn illustration for this first Royal Tiger brochure because there were no bodied vehicles to photograph.

For any operators wary about maintaining a vehicle with the engine hidden under the floor, Leyland optimistically says: "If necessary, the complete engine unit can be removed, replaced and started up in under 50 minutes." That I'd like to see,

Around the same time Tilling-Stevens, by then no longer a significant force in the bus and coach business, produced a brochure for the Express Mark II medium weight coach. There's a detailed

Luxury at Low Cost

THE NEW RANGE OF

BEDFORD

PASSENGER
VEHICLES

WITH COACHWORK BY

DUPLE

Falcon

PASSENGER CHASSIS

DENNIS BROS LTD GUILDFORD

specification, but no mention of the gross vehicle weight to explain what "medium weight" actually means. This had a pretty painting on the cover (7) of a coach on a bright coastal road with white cliffs in the background and seagulls wheeling overhead. There will be seagulls over the white cliffs of Dover?

No, doesn't sound quite right. But the pastel colours help conjure up thoughts of relaxed summer touring.

The chassis came with a full-width dash panel and under the heading "Beauty of line", Tilling-Stevens has this to say: "The modern but dignified frontal design of the Tilling-Stevens chassis lends itself to a continuity of line which enables the coach to be planned on up-to-date principles pleasing to the eye and practical in its fullest sense." I'm not sure what that last phrase means, but you get the message.

In 1950 Foden elected to use spot colour for an advert in *Commercial Motor*, the weekly magazine (8). The bus was a 1948 delivery to West Wales of Tycroes, and was illustrated against a backdrop of Caerphilly Castle, home of bodybuilder Welsh Metal Industries, a company which had a penchant for building angular bus bodies. The spot colour was blue; West Wales' buses were not.

Daimler introduced its underfloor-engined bus chassis, the Freeline, in 1951, and for a brochure published soon after the launch commissioned an illustration of a coach with a Duple Roadmaster body against a vague backdrop of big city buildings (9). The pink, black and cream livery was an unusual choice.

Neither the Freeline nor the Roadmaster were a great success. In contrast the combination of Bedford and Duple was a winner, and in the 1950s Bedford's coach chassis was the SB, which really did offer luxury at low cost, as this 1952 brochure promised. Bedford's copywriter waxed lyrical, talking of "the

17

Bus & Coach

MAY 1956 · VOL. 28 NO. 5 · TWO SHILLINGS AND SIXPENCE

CROSSLEY
58 – Seater Metal Framed Double
Deck Bus in Service with Liverpool
Corporation.

501 LIME ST LIMITED STOP

P.R.V. GROUP BODY SALES DIVISION

PARK ROYAL VEHICLES LTD. ABBEY ROAD. LONDON. N.W.10.
TELEPHONE: ELGAR 6522

smoothness, silkiness and silence of its big, six cylinder petrol engine" before talking about cruising with "no more than a gentle murmur, as unobtrusive as the engine of a big saloon car".

Where Daimler went for a stylised backdrop, Bedford's SB with Duple Vega body is clearly on an Alpine tour with a dramatic viewpoint (10). It carries the artist's signature, Noel McVeigh, who also worked for Vauxhall.

During the 1950s there was really no competition for Bedford in the lightweight coach market. Among those

who tried was Dennis, with its 7-ton GVW Falcon, a high-framed front-engined chassis not to be confused with the 1980s low-framed rear-engined urban bus.

A 1952 Dennis brochure features an atmospheric painting of a 1951 Duple-bodied Falcon, MPT 640, operated by General of Chester-le-Street (11). It is based on a black-and-white photograph which is shown inside the brochure, but with brightly-lit interior detail, including some out-of-scale passengers. But what are they doing in this strange and slightly threatening world? Are they lost? It's all a bit spooky...

Where Dennis's artist has carefully added realistic colour to an original photo, the same hasn't happened at Burlingham, with a May 1953 advert in the *Leyland Journal* celebrating trips from north-west England to London for the coronation (12). Purple was the colour Leyland had chosen for the cover of this issue of its customer magazine (perhaps because of its royal connotations), and Burlingham has used it to doubtful effect to represent the red livery used by Ribble, whose fleetname has been added in a rather amateur fashion. In fact the coach is unlikely to be one of the 15 Royal Tigers delivered to Ribble in 1953 as it is probable that none were completed in time to be photographed for this advert. The glazed panels on the front dome read Burlingham Seagull, suggesting a demonstrator. The juxtaposition of Blackpool Tower with the Victoria Memorial which stands in front of Buckingham Palace is a nice touch.

London provides part of the backdrop for a Strachans Everest brochure (13). The Everest name was a topical choice, as climbers had reached the peak of the Himalayan mountain for the first time in 1953. Strachans described its new coach body as "The peak of perfection". The painting sets the coach in Trafalgar Square, and from the left you can see the base of Nelson's column, the steeple of St Martin-in-the-Fields, and towers of the London Coliseum and the National Gallery. And appearing as a ghostly presence in the background above St Martin-in-the-Fields is a faint representation of Mount Everest.

The Everest name was used for a number of Strachans bodies which were generally more angular than this illustration suggests.

A 1955 brochure from AEC (14) has a painting by Leslie Carr, a prolific poster artist whose work included commissions for railway companies and car manufacturers. On the right is a Reliance coach with bodywork by Roe. And in the background is an integral AEC-Park Royal Monocoach. The setting is suitably English, hinting at old cities like Canterbury and York. The use of an unusual Roe Dalesman coach might at first seem odd in a world dominated by Duple and Plaxton. But the explanation is simple. Roe was a sister company of AEC in the Associated Commercial Vehicles group.

In the 1950s and 1960s Duple produced an Annual which illustrated the company's current range with, in 1955, a mixture of black-and-white photographs and colour illustrations. It also contained adverts from the company's suppliers and dealers. This is an Elizabethan (15), with Buckingham Palace in the background (and the Victoria Monument, last seen with Burlingham in 1953). It's a charming illustration, even if the proportions and the perspective are a bit suspect. The registration, DUP 54, indicates Duple 1954.

Duple's text describes the Elizabethan as a "majestic coach" - nice pun – and says it can be fitted to "all makes of underfloor engine chassis, including AEC Reliance and Mark IV, Leyland Royal Tiger and Tiger Cub, Daimler Freeline, Dennis Falcon and Lancet, Guy Arab, Atkinson, Seddon MkXI, and Sentinel". Adapting the body for even half of that list would have kept Duple's drawing office busy.

The Annual's opening page includes directions to Duple's factory and offices in The Hyde, Hendon and these include the advice: "Buses 60, 83, 142 and 183 and Green Line Coaches 706, 707, 708 pass the door." The 83 still serves The Hyde, but Duple's factory has long since gone.

Meanwhile Daimler in its 1955 brochure for "The new CVG double deck chassis" used this dramatic illustration (16) to tell the world it was exporting chassis. The brochure is quite a lavish production, but with no colour photography – just the use of yellow and red ink to liven it up. The illustration has been reproduced by an artist copying a photograph, and it shows a chassis being unloaded from a ship at an un-named port.

The vessel on the left has the word "Castle" on the bow as the second part of its two-part name (the first part is deliberately indecipherable) which suggests the Union-Castle Line, whose main routes were from the UK to South Africa. But that's not where this is. Indeed, the "Castle" might be a red herring. Yet wherever it is, the use of colour adds power to an image which would be much less interesting without it. And, as so often with commercial illustration, there's no indication of the artist's name.

An unusual method of producing colour illustrations for adverts was used by Park Royal in the mid 1950s: collage. The picture of the Liverpool Corporation Crossley-bodied AEC Regent V (17) is a fine example of a hand-coloured black-and-white

print. But the figures on the left and on the right foreground, also hand coloured, have been cut out of another photograph and pasted in place. So, too, has the last seated passenger on the upper deck. It's a measure of the skill of the artist, identified only as R de P, that you can't see the join. For other adverts R de P used a cut-out image of a bus, which was then stuck on to a painted backdrop, as illustrated by an East Kent Guy Arab in a rural scene with oasthouses (18). The bus was photographed in black-and-white – probably at the Park Royal factory – and R de P has added not just colour, but passengers and a driver too. It is a superb creation and - dare I say it? - nicer than any colour photograph.

Back in 1952 Bedford showed a coach in the Alps. In 1958 it showed a Duple Super Vega, delivering sophisticated patrons to the upmarket Hotel Imperial (19). There was a Hotel Imperial in London in 1958, but it looked nothing like this, so the entire setting might be pure artistry.

Coach styling had changed dramatically in just six years, but Duple reassures prospective buyers: "Up to the minute in contemporary continental styling this coach will retain the 'new look' long after other present-day designs have become outdated."

The driver has a white top on his peaked cap, although I do wonder why he's not outside the coach helping his passengers alight – and ready to collect a tip... The lilac and pink livery is imaginative.

As the 1950s drew to a close, the use of hand-coloured black-and-white images and of original painted illustrations declined as a growing number of automotive manufacturers used real colour photographs to illustrate their products. Reality was taking over from fantasy. But when you look back at the best of the 1950s illustrations, you appreciate that skilled artists were creating idealised images with an aura of romance which no camera could ever match. ■

BEDFORD-DUPLE COACHES FOR 1959

19

Seen in October 2008, an Alexander ALX400-bodied Dennis Trident of Travel London approaches the modest apex of the almost invisible bridge that carries Wimbledon Broadway over the mainline railway between Croydon and central London.

OVER AND UNDER

All photographs by the author.

Sometimes you see them, sometimes you don't, but bridges feature in a surprising number of bus photographs. **Peter Rowlands** reflects on the way they can add drama to the result – assuming you can find the ideal shooting position.

Bridges have a strange role in bus photography. The more striking examples can give extraordinary presence to a picture, not to mention providing natural framing and open space. Yet in other instances they hardly seem to merit any remark. For this article I delved through my archives, looking for photographs in which bridges represented a key component, and I was surprised to find just how many there were. Beam bridges, arch bridges, cantilever bridges, cable-stayed bridges – seemingly they're everywhere.

Understandably, you might think first of iconic bridges – those that clamour to feature in any photograph taken in the vicinity: Tower Bridge in London, the Tyne Bridge between Newcastle and Gateshead, the Transporter Bridge in Teesside. They define their area, and immediately give context to

ABOVE: **January 2010 brought snow in unfamiliar quantities to west London. This Optare-bodied Dennis Trident of London General approaches Putney bridge station from the south.**

any bus photograph. They introduce drama.

However, plenty of less high-profile bridges also end up featuring in many bus photographs; and that applies even to underbridges that are almost invisible unless you're looking for them – bridges that carry the road over a river, a railway or a natural depression. Often they're level with the road that runs across them, and may be flanked by walls that half-conceal whatever passes beneath them. (Another road? A railway? A culvert?)

Sometimes, though, the bridge rises a little in the middle – offering an irresistible opportunity for a dramatic low-angle photograph as a bus reaches the apex.

Even bridges that don't stand out in this way can often be a compelling lure for photographers. There are usually no buildings on bridges, so you can capture the bus without having to contend with too much clutter. Moreover, the light is often brighter, and there are fewer shadows at the end of the day
or the year.

Overbridges too can sometimes seem almost invisible. Maybe they're just footbridges or parts of buildings; maybe they're so familiar that we almost ignore them. Yet they can still offer a dramatic frame for a picture of a bus passing under them.

Yet buses on bridges are not necessarily easy photographic targets. If you're shooting a bus on or close to the bridge itself, you won't usually be able to stand very far back from the road – not unless the pavement is generously wide. So you may well find yourself taking head-on shots when you'd have preferred a three-quarters view.

Sometimes you can cheat, of course. Putney bridge in west London, for instance, has refuges set into the side walls at regular intervals. If you position yourself in one of these to photograph a bus on the bridge, the photograph can make it appear that you were floating somewhere over the river when you took the picture, beyond the side of the bridge.

However, another facet of bridges is that they can be pinch points. All traffic is forced to pass over them, and that will often include pedestrians. Here comes the bus you want to photograph ... but here comes a clutch of shoppers. Will they reach the point where you've lined up your photograph before or after the bus? Should you claim your shooting position and maintain it obstinately as they approach? Should you choose the street side of the pavement or the river side? What if one of the pedestrians is pushing a pram-load of triplets, and

ABOVE: **Routemaster RML 2452, then in the Arriva South London fleet, comes to rest just after crossing Battersea Bridge in March 2005, not long before the route was converted to one-person operation. It was later preserved.**

ABOVE: **Soft afternoon sun shines on this Plaxton President-bodied Volvo B7TL of London General as it crosses Vauxhall bridge from Victoria in October 2004.**

can't pass unless you get out of the way?

A quirk of British road bridges is that few of them have a name that is generally known. Instead, they often simply share the name of the road that runs over them, or have a colloquial name, typically describing the river they are crossing. No doubt the local authority will have its own designation for every one of them, but it's surprising how seldom this is shared with the general public.

Yet named or not, bridges are an intrinsic part of the built landscape, and an invaluable contributor to the photographic record. ∎

ABOVE: **A Leyland Titan on route 78 pulls away from Tower bridge in June 1986, when it was only two years old. It joined the Stagecoach fleet in 1994, and was transferred to Stagecoach Fife four years later.**

BELOW: **A Volvo B10M with Alexander PS bus body in the fleet of First Glasgow, seen in Argyll Street after passing under the imposing Glasgow Central Station bridge in September 2008.**

ABOVE: **This dual-door ECW-bodied Leyland Atlantean of Go-Ahead Northern heads south over the Tyne Bridge towards Whickham in April 1987.**

ABOVE: **Back in the 1980s, it seemed for a while that every regional bus operator wanted ex-London Routemasters. This one ran for United Counties before Stagecoach corporate livery took hold, and is seen in Bedford heading north across the River Great Ouse in May 1988.**

ABOVE: **In July 1989 York City & District was the branding used for buses running in York for the former NBC West Yorkshire operation. This Mark 2 Leyland National is crossing the River Ouse on Lower Ousegate.**

BELOW: **An ex-Eastern Counties Bristol VRT wearing pale blue Cambus livery crosses the Cam on Victoria Avenue, Cambridge, in August 1985. In the background is Midsummer Common. The bus was new to Maidstone & District in 1974.**

ABOVE: **Similar angle, different shade of blue for this January 1985 view of a Bristol VRT of Great Yarmouth Corporation with ECW body built at nearby Lowestoft. It is heading west on Bridge Street – one of only two bridges in the town crossing the River Yare.**

BELOW LEFT: **Part of the Runcorn Busway features an elevated roadway – in effect an extended bridge. A Leyland National 2 of Crosville is seen here in what was then called the Shopping City area in March 1985. Most of the 1971-built busway is still in use.**

BELOW: **Like many operators, Lincolnshire Road Car embraced midibuses in the privatisation era. This MCW Metrorider is seen crossing the River Witham on Broadgate, Lincoln in August 1997, with the cathedral looming in the background.**

ABOVE: **These Alexander-bodied Dennis Dominators provide a reminder of the colourful Mainline livery adopted by South Yorkshire in 1989. They are seen in Sheffield's Haymarket in September 1997, by which time the operator was in FirstBus ownership. The footbridge behind them celebrates the Castlegate market and shopping area, now being redeveloped.**

An MCW-bodied Leyland Atlantean of the Tyne and Wear PTE pulls away from Wearmouth bridge, Sunderland in August 1986, against the background of the railway bridge now used by the Metro.

The changing fortunes of the bus station

Robert E. Jowitt provides a catalogue of origins, varieties and vagaries of establishments from Cam to Itchen and Colne to Usk.

A s the late 1920s moved towards the early 1930s, the Jazz Era towards Depression, and buses edged from almost equine primitive aura towards streamlined sophistication, there could be observed here and there in the streets of English towns and cities diverse respectable-looking gents whose Argus-eyed mien and habit would have been likely, 15 years earlier, to have had them arrested in anti-alien-spy-hysterical-phobia. Enemies, however, they were not. They were merely minions gathering evidence for the looming cloud of the forthcoming Road Traffic Bill, although this in itself caused an alarm and hatred – almost equal to earlier xenophobia – in the hearts and minds of honest omnibus operators who had in perfectly satisfactory fashion been managing their affairs in their own way for the past decade or even in some cases from before the outbreak of the First World War.

RIGHT: **This doleful acre is, if anywhere positive, somewhere near Bearwood west of Birmingham, a stop, layover and probably terminus for Birmingham Coach Company Leyland Nationals. That it could be called a bus station is debatable, but the scene is a score of years ago, and perhaps it has been cleaned up since.**

ABOVE: **Halesowen in the 1990s, bright with diverse denizens of the Black Country, notably Ludlows second-hand Nationals.**

After the Bill became the Act, nevertheless, the wisdom of it gradually became apparent, as the anarchy of excessive competition was ironed out, the London General and its manifold multi-hued opponents all merged into red London Transport, and multiple coach firms rivalling each other with fare wars over the same route vastly and in orderly manner reduced, while chaotic performances on unsuitable or virtually impossible stopping places in ancient city streets were largely eradicated, in the

TOP RIGHT: **Colchester, February 1991, with an Eastern National National nestled under the multi-story car park.**

BELOW RIGHT: **The bus layover area viewed from the top of Colchester's multi-story car-park. On the left an ex-Blackpool Atlantean with Norfolk; on the right an ex-Tayside Fleetline with Osborne.**

LOWER RIGHT: **Southampton in the early 1970s, the H&D Bus Station lay-over fringe, a scene to gladden Bristol lovers' hearts.**

course of time, by the excellent notion of purpose-built off-street bus stations.

It must of course be admitted that the idea was not new, for carrier's cart men moving into the motor era in many cases continued to use the yards of ale-houses and taverns which served the rural treks of their fathers before them, and the great concerns, seeing the burgeoning internal-combustion entry as a useful and economic expansion to the glorious spread of electric traction, indulged handsomely in the spirit of the sport, witness particularly the ornamental ironwork, crowned by British Electric Traction's sparking magnet, at Durham Bus Station.

The Road Traffic Act simply provided a tremendous boost or fillip to the bus station conception, and this emerged in various forms and purposes. Some stations were almost exclusively the domain of cross-country express and ad-hoc excursions and tours, others again devoted to local and longer services of one particular company (perhaps with a dash of infiltration from some other such firm allowed by a "gentlemen's agreement"), while yet another variant allowed a host of small peripheral rustics to grab a bay here and there in the new paradise replacing the pot-house yard, and the great cities and municipalities stuck in large measure to their privilege of loading and unloading their tram passengers in the middle of the road and the bus passengers on the pavement as tradition with almost Biblical sanction demanded.

The architecture was as varied as the purpose, some establishments proving boldly avant-garde with perhaps an influence of art-deco and Palm Beach, while others proved little better than more-or-less practical specimens of the multiple hut or henhouse encampment. Post-Hitler-War, when the merits of the bus station still held sway in planning eyes, there emanated from architects' drawing boards bold schemes of heroically hideous design known as brutalism and similar terms, deemed suitable for the passage of buses and the dalliance of their passengers, receiving mingled extravagant praise and damning disgust in the pages of architectural journals and other such print where intelligentsia and cognoscenti give opinion on the ways of the world.

Whatever their style it did strike me, and had done from my early youth, that the buses in them, and come to that in the countryside around and about, were all exactly the same, all Bristol, and all the same green or the same red. From Lands End to East Anglia, from North Wales to Hampshire, although there were interesting variants from Southdown to Ribble via Midland Red. Honestly I did not take

LEFT: **After the closure and demolition of Southampton H&D Bus Station, stops sprang up on many lengths of pavement with croquet hoops as the first stages of shelters, in July 1987; but they were all gone again not much more than a decade later.**

much notice, just accepted the scene as it stood and appeared as if it would stand for ever, while I stuck to my Continental trams.

Then, although I still didn't follow the political ins and outs, it started to be a bit different. You could not help noticing it was all called National, and running Leyland National buses besides. National started to jazz up matters a little, under some scheme which, so I was told, was Market Analysis Project or MAP for short, which involved adding local names to sections of the large units and of revamped lettering in a new image, but not much improvement after years of neglect which had probably started to infiltrate with post-war nationalization.

Such case applied particularly to bus stations and must have impelled anyone who could afford a car to avoid such fag-smoke-scented hell-holes

of cloth-capped workers and mums screeching at undisciplined kids. Presumably they were failing to realise that they were grid-locking not only the buses they despised but themselves too.

While MAP may be deemed to have been a step in the right direction, and an indication that thought and care were directed to the subject, a far more vastly drastic change swept onto the scene in the last quarter of the century with the Iron Lady's grand notions of privatization. I had severe doubts about privatization of both railways and buses. On the railways, surely it should revert to some time more like pre-1948 or even before 1923. The idea of one party owning the track and another the rolling stock seemed to me unsatisfactory and even unsafe (hasn't this proved true?) while the buses were to revert to pre-Road Traffic Act days and abandon a system which, if fraying a little at the edges, had held most adequate sway for half a century.

I was neither in a position nor interested enough to follow the cases in any great detail, being for most of that period in rural Herefordshire. Admittedly

BELOW: **With bus station gone in Southampton, buses couldn't help bad manners. A Solent Blue flat-windscreen VR has to mount the pavement to pass halted Hampshire Bus Bristols.**

ABOVE: **The BET sparking magnet over the Omnibus Station in Durham, c1966.**

ABOVE: **Newport, Mon, in 1986. The bus shelters, of enormous length, are neither straight nor level.**

Hereford itself was, so I am told, a pioneer site for introducing the "let 'em all come" practice, but by the time I came to drive Primrose buses from Leominster into its streets the affair seemed to have settled down into a flood of Hereford Hopper Midland-Red-derived minibuses noticeable to me only as I might notice a swarm of buzzing annoying flies (save only that you can't swat a Hopper even with a battered Primrose Ford.) Anyway they had their own Hopper station, with a tiny Hopper-size roundabout, passably sensible in a Tesco grand plan, while the country bus station slightly further out of town was, so far as I could tell, much as it must have been for many years, with a fine variety of independents at windswept platforms.

The only hitch was that one Primrose service, albeit Saturdays only, was scheduled to enter also the Hopper station and not infrequently fell to me with, due to schools out-stationing, a 53-seater, no joke squashed among the flies…

At Leominster, the other end of the routes I drove, the bus station was for years two double-sided islands in what could once have been the market, while a new bus station of similar ground plan but smarter intention across the road served for several years as car-park for a new supermarket next door, until at last the buses gained their rights…

From this starting point I intend to stray in vaguely coherent geographical directions, though not again as far north as Durham, through various other bus stations which I knew for better or worse. My readers will have their own favourite – or despised – spots and I may annoy them because I cannot – or will not – mention such as I never reached. To some of those I did I must pay brief homage or, betimes, abuse.

In truth the only major city I visited with any frequency in those early deregulated years, once I had moved from Hampshire and the buses familiar all my life was Birmingham.

The Black Country I had known in the days when there were dark blue and cream Corporation buses in Birmingham, and green and cream trolleybuses in Wolverhampton and pale blue trolleybuses in Walsall. Walsall trolleybuses - and motor buses - enjoyed quite a generous bus station, Wolverhampton, less so, and neither very conducive to suffering Midlands rain.

But the Birmingham Midland Red bus station, roofed all over, was of such dingy darkness that you might think yourself waiting for Charon, the Ferryman of the Dead, on the banks of the River Styx, rather than for a common bus to Ludlow. On the way to Ludlow there was a place on the edge of

BELOW: **Bath is one of Europe's most elegant cities, but the bus station is most uninspiring concrete.**

ABOVE: **Hereford, several windswept parallel lines with dingy shelters, possibly inadequately seated? Scene 1997, but with bright array of elderly rustics could have been years earlier.**

ABOVE: **In Marlands, Southampton, spring 2009, the building behind the Optare Spectra is on the site of the H&D bus station.**

Birmingham which may have been counted a bus station as it allowed buses a sensibly large area to turn or stop off the road, but it could claim otherwise only the poorest of shelters and heaps of debris. Halesowen was much brighter, with more stands and better shelters. Ludlows Buzz With Us Leyland Nationals and several other outfits added to the gaiety.

You returned to gloom in Kidderminster, while in Ludlow itself, where no Ludlows Buzz With Us ever penetrated, the stops were time-honoured roadside kerbs, apart from about three white-lined slots at the end of the market place for rustics. The streets of Birmingham, blue-bussed in Corporation or WMPTE, likewise allowed their kerbs to serve for a vast majority of routes... and for other colours besides blue.

Cheltenham Coach Station was of course famous as a Black & White paradise, and I regret I never properly sampled it until its glory was already rather tarnished or, as I might say, National white. Bristol

was another all-over roof and mildly reminiscent of Birmingham but somehow less lugubriously dank and dark inside. Along the road Bath claimed a monolith with saw-tooth bays ranged below, hardly worthy of one of the most elegant cities in the country.

Up Severn, in Worcester, back towards the Black Country, buses left a large pit-like arena of bus-stops to pass under a shopping complex. This, like Hereford Hoppers, made some town-centre convenient sense; there may have been a Midland Red West finger in the pie here too.

Far to the east, but going a bit underground again, the approach to Colchester bus station was through what could be described as the undercroft or cellar of a multi-story car-park, a juxtaposition I felt rather paradoxical. Sudbury, up the map a bit, was home to thoroughly independent rurally-inclined East Anglians in little better than a back-street yard, scantly protected from East Anglian ill weather, and not over well informed about which buses might go where. It was at least not far from the centre. Up the map again, Wymondham, about the same size as Sudbury, provides simple pavement stops in the main square, this adorned with lovely circular market house of 1618 on stilts, a charming scene.

Not far away is Norwich, a vague bus station near the old City Wall which I saw only from a distance, and the main stops for many outfits all along both sides of the broad street below the Castle, thoroughly traditional. I read that Norwich lately gained a new fairly central "state-of-the-art" bus station; an Anglian driver I met the other day told me it is too small.

In Cambridge National Express terminates at shelters below handsome trees next a slightly agoraphobic spread of greensward named Parker's Piece, slightly further from the centre than you might reckon a comfortable walk; but not half so far as the railway station which definitely demands a bus and has a row of stops and shelter to answer fairly close by. The Bus Station proper is in Drummer Street, and though but one long shelter with buses at right-angles and some paucity of home comfort or information it is redeemed and flanked by a very pleasant nobly-treed park named Christ's Pieces (yes, plural, not like Parker) and useful proximity to town and gown. It is the place for rural and interurban buses, including those denizens guided by the former railway track to St Ives. The city bus services all have their halting places hereabouts old-time at the pavements, sometimes decidedly frenetically.

The guided busway goes to St Ives where a former cattle market with fine gateways makes an antisocial bus station on a winter Sunday nearing dusk, mildly less daunting at other seasons. Onwards unguided to Huntingdon where the bus station is nondescript to unmemorable.

Back westwards, to that boldest and most magic range of hills where Malvern hangs, a series of ledges, on the eastern flank of the spine. Where all is very steep Midland Red had only a long lay-by on the main road with a string of dark thin antique shelters and glimpses more or less level to the top of the abbey tower, the abbey being on the ledge below. From here sideways up the hills to the pass at Upper Wyche, a grand view west to the Black Mountains, then down through rich farmland to Ledbury. Here, at an early age, I was much struck by the bizarre appearance of the skinny-half-cab Midland Red single-deckers, halting on street next the C17th town hall, rectangular, larger than, but on legs like Wymondham, rendering an equally jolly bus-in-townscape picture. I believe that the situation still prevails, though not with those half-cabs.

Another Midland Red hop – through hop-fields(!) – takes us back to Hereford, then by independent

ABOVE: **Newport, IoW, 2005, seen through a Dennis Dart on the stop at west end of the bus station are, right, the central island for two or three stops and, left, the copious lay-over space.**

over a pastoral carpet to Monmouth where buses seem to stop and wait vaguely in side streets rather than in the square under the statue of Rolls (as in Royce) holding an early air-plane, as would seem to me more suitable. Onwards down the dramatic Wye gorge to Chepstow and bus station of three or four angled slots on a broad section of road, perhaps post-war widening for the purpose, not far from the city gate. Here the Wye joins the Severn; downstream the Usk does likewise. Up the Usk is Newport, Mon.

Here is (or was?) the most weird but perhaps most appealing bus station of all. Parallel tunnel-like shelters stretched, though not entirely straight, over an undulating surface for what seemed at least a quarter of a mile, with gaps in the glazed sides at the bus stops but roofed all the way. To add to this quaint scene the stops were served in many cases by Metro-Scanias. These are long gone; is the rest too?

The other Newport, ie Isle of Wight, had Vectis buses councilled-out from a time-honoured terminus in the central St James Square into a purpose-built concrete affair nearby in 1962 with one long roof along one side and a median strip of shelters, 12 stands in all, plus saw-tooth lay-over parking for 24 buses on the north side, and useful offices for staff, café and waiting room and small but convenience-friendly shops for passengers. The roof, it has to be said, rendered the pavement below rather dim. Over the edifice flew a Southern Vectis flag. I shall return hither in a moment in the final development of my argument. Still on the South Coast the shoe-box architecture and saw-tooth stops at Poole are claimed by some to be the most dismal and depressing bus station in England. Fareham could

In hope of escaping from
Staines, 2010.

was done to match this effort, decay continued.

These last ten years or more, in wet weather, buses at the stands can be surrounded by puddles reaching to all four wheels, making boarding an art. All this time planners and developers have wrangled, and as I write in the spring of 2016 they wrangle still while desolation could inspire bleak poetry. If they do knock it down and the truth of a myth that OMNIBUS

boast little better than a yard and huts, Gosport, so far as I remember, just a yard (though matters are improved now, and buses between the two latter can hurtle along their own private ex-railway road before joining the traffic jams of Gosport).

After those Argus-eyed gents had spied out the land in Winchester the city was provided with a fine but rather out-of-town Coach Station, Hants & Dorset built their own Bus Station adjacent to the Broadway, and King Alfred stuck firmly to the Broadway pavements. The Coach Station proudly housed an elevated signal-box with signalman displaying illuminated numbers to bid express coaches into the parallel bays next it and touring coaches into the right-angle bays on the flanks; I never counted how many bays made up the full complement but it may have been more than 40. On summer Sundays in my youth in the 1950s constant in-and-out traffic kept them pretty full.

The Hants & Dorset bus station was ornamented with a portal bearing a fine inscription of the company title and OMNIBUS STATION. Behind this brave frontage matters were rather less inspiring with blank brick walls, barely adequate roofs, and murky enquiry office leading to smoky café. A workshop, not un-handsome for its period, formed the backdrop. With MAP and like whimsicalities in the 1970s and 1980s OMNIBUS STATION was replaced in heavy-serif trendy letters saying WINCHESTER BUS STATION. Little or nothing inside

survives behind the board of no-longer trendy serif is proved, (the latter letters have dropped off or been thrown away leaving mere shadows of their former selves,) let us pray a dollop of preservation wisdom will prevail. As to what will happen to the buses...

It seems that the Coach Station was too far away from city centre. National Express and tour coaches now load and unload among the old King Alfred stops in the Broadway and among the buses which in many guises these past 40 years have replaced the heroes of antiquity. Even though empty tour coaches go on to park in the remains of the signal-box-less coach station, the chaos in the Broadway is exactly such as Traffic Commissioners were deploring 85 years ago. Add the bus station traffic to this, and the worthy men will be turning in their graves.

Speaking as a mere bystander – and I admit that what I say herewith are my own opinions and not intended to malign any particular party - privatisation did, as I see it, bring some merits, especially in the form of so called management buy-outs, where huge unfeeling concerns with all the apathy of the post-war Atlee nationalisation were broken up into smaller outfits run by people with genuine enthusiasm for and knowledge of the job they were undertaking, and provided well-conceived and useful services.

The ugly side was that all too often large firms, albeit private, acquired large chunks of operating territory for profit rather than practical provision for passengers, and employed abacus-counters from vague college courses rather than experienced men who had grown up on the road; though I hasten to add that many of the younger generation of my acquaintance in the industry are no mere number-crunching whizz-kids while among the older members are certain hidebound reactionaries who cannot or will not adapt to sensible progress. All in all, the overall private situation, mostly huge groups, was little better than before, worse where unremunerative services were abandoned, and worse still where bus stations were sold for development.

Southern Vectis travelled from management buy-out to sell-out to Go Ahead, and those useful bus parking spaces in Newport became a row of shops and, in a much smaller (as Norwich!) bus station behind, still a decent waiting room and staff quarters but only about six stands and six lay-over spaces. So buses had to squeeze past each other and drive out and round the shops to wait for space. Parts of the surface succumbed to subsequent subsidence taking weeks to rectify, confusion worse confounded. That flag wasn't flown any more either.

The case of Hants & Dorset in Southampton was even more dire, for the whole huge bus station was laid waste for superstores, and bus stops sprung up instead on every available kerb stone, forcing moving buses into unseemly tactics to pass halted ones. In the Bible is a famous tale of Esau selling his birthright to his brother for a mess of pottage. "More fool him," some might reasonably say. Bus management could usefully read this bit of scripture…

Thus far in this catalogue we have been skirting London, albeit erratically, at between 50 and 100 or more miles. We now turn towards the capital, via Guildford; here the Bus Station is long and thin with architecturally curious shelter, along most of the west side, partly, where it curves, built to match the saw-teeth below. On the east side one long island

shelter of profile rather like those plate-layers' concrete huts formerly familiar on the Southern Railway, the business side of the island being on the public highway while station side is just layovers. The whole surrounded by dismal backsides of unidentified modernism - or dereliction awaiting demolition and development?

Then Staines, pretty wide open, shelters just adequate, but protected from presumed west wind by multi-story car-park and, if I remember right, a shopping mall. Until recently Slough was roofed all over, maybe to provide shelter from friendly bombs, adjacent to a monstrosity of shoebox style named inappropriately after Brunel. This, I am told, is gone, passengers and the entrances of the buses sheltered by a stylish feature known as 'the Wave'. Let us end up in Euston, where, about the site of the vandal destruction of the renowned Doric Arch, in and out under the motley frightfulness which replaced it, a huge number of buses come and go constantly, vastly heartening in their purposeful thriving.

Buses are sufficiently vital to our lives that they deserve better treatment - their passengers likewise - far too seldom afforded. Even if Norwich is too small it marks a forward step; and there are in all probability further examples of new or at least rejuvenated thinking on this issue, unknown to me. I can't go everywhere nor read every word of bus-press news, I just hope that the souls of those long-deceased Commissioners may find some measure of appeasement. ∎

BOTH BOTTOM: **Winchester, with the 1930s Hants & Dorset Omnibus Station frontage, and then the later, less grand, remodelled version. The earlier picture dates from the early 1970s and shows the mayor inspecting the men of the Royal Greenjackets being given the Freedom of the City, and (presumably as a temporary measure) the entrance of the bus station.**

In June 1977, West Midlands PTE dual-door Leyland National 4798 (KOM 798P) in its patriotic NEC livery is inbound from the south car parks. The background area has since changed significantly. After the NEC contract was lost to National Travel West, the Nationals gained standard fleet livery but were taken out of service in the run up to deregulation.

Serving the NEC – the first decade

David Cole takes a look at the variety of operators and vehicles engaged in moving visitors from the car parks to the exhibition halls at Britain's biggest exhibition centre.

When the queen opened Birmingham's National Exhibition Centre in February 1976, it marked a new direction for the exhibition industry in the UK. Prior to the NEC, most national exhibitions were shoehorned into inner city sites, well connected transport-wise but short on space. The NEC changed all this, built on a greenfield site close to the motorway network and designed with the car driving visitor in mind.

The development initially consisted of five halls surrounded by green space and large outlying car parks, distant enough to require a shuttle bus service to move visitors from the car parks to the NEC's central Piazza. With local authority involvement in developing the site, it was perhaps not surprising that their operator, the West Midlands PTE, was initially tasked with providing the shuttle buses. For this purpose, twelve dual-doorway 11.3m Leyland Nationals were acquired and finished in a patriotic red, white and blue colour scheme. When not required at the NEC, they appeared at times on local bus routes around Solihull.

LEFT: **At the first NEC Motor Show in September 1978, National Travel West provided the internal car park shuttles with vehicles drawn from a wide area. Plaxton Supreme-bodied Bedford YMT YUE 595S had joined the fleet in the Midlands in the previous May.**

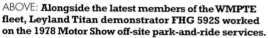

ABOVE: **Alongside the latest members of the WMPTE fleet, Leyland Titan demonstrator FHG 592S worked on the 1978 Motor Show off-site park-and-ride services.**

The big prize for the NEC was enticing the Motor Show out of London, and this started with the first combined car and commercial show in October 1978. By this time, the car park shuttle contract had passed to National Travel West using high-floor coaches. They were more comfortable but not exactly the quickest or easiest to load for the short journeys involved. The attendance at the biennial Motor Show was expected to be well beyond the capacity of the site's own car parks, especially when most of one car park would be taken up by visiting coaches.

The result was the introduction of a wide-ranging off-site park-and-ride operation using fleets of mainly double-deckers linking in to a temporary bus station. In 1978, WMPTE provided this with many

TOP RIGHT: **Midland Red Express operations in 1982 featured a range of support vehicles creating a virtual depot at the NEC. The AEC Matador recovery vehicle normally based at Digbeth depot was bodied in house by Midland Red and now survives in preservation.**

BELOW: **Immortalised in model form by EFE, the 1966 AEC Mammoth Major tanker KGY 808D was acquired secondhand by Midland Red from Shell Mex BP when disruption to the company's fuel supply was expected.**

ABOVE RIGHT: **Already toilet-equipped, Plaxton Elite-bodied Leyland Leopard 312 (PHA 312M) was fitted with tables for use as a drivers' rest room. The coach had already spent nine hard years shuttling up and down the M1.**

RIGHT: **Still carrying National Travel West legal lettering, former Ribble Leyland Titan PD3 with Burlingham body, KCK 918, was at the centre of operations complete with power and communication connections.**

recently-delivered Daimler Fleetlines supported by the pre-production MCW Metrobuses and Leyland Titans also new that year. By 1982, when the off-site operation probably reached its zenith, the recently-created Midland Red Express company, as successor to National Travel West, hired in vehicles from a number of operators including Midland Red North, Midland Red East and PMT. The batch of MAN artics delivered to the South Yorkshire PTE also featured before moving on loan to Midland Red West. Later these would pass to Midland Red North and would again be seen at the NEC.

Some of the park-and-ride sites were a distance away with one in 1978 being on an unopened stretch of the M42 motorway near Coleshill. The operation was supported by a virtual depot on the still loosely-surfaced NEC West Car Park, offering recovery, fuelling and driver rest facilities as well a control point. Passenger facilities were limited and it would not have been a pleasant experience on the, from

ABOVE: **MAN introduced the SG192 articulated bus to the UK in 1978. Demonstrator CLM 346T worked for National Travel West on the car park shuttles during the 1978 Motor Show before becoming one of five similar vehicles to join the South Yorkshire PTE fleet. Displaced from their Sheffield City Clipper duties after less than three years, all five were used by Midland Red Express on the 1982 Motor Show off-site park-and-ride services prior to spending a year with Midland Red West in Redditch.**

BOTTOM LEFT: **2003 (DAK 303V) is shown rounding junction 6 of the M42 still carrying SYPTE legal lettering.**

BELOW: **In 1984, they joined the Midland Red North fleet and were to put in a final appearance at the NEC on the 1986 Motor Show car park shuttles. Renumbered 1802, DAK 302V is seen departing the NEC Piazza. The following year all but the former demonstrator were exported to Australia, the demonstrator meeting its end in a Barnsley scrapyard.**

memory thankfully few, wet days.

When the NEC reached its tenth birthday, plans were advancing for a significant expansion of the site to which The Forum, a small standalone hall and The Arena had already been added together with more car parks. Shows and their requirements were changing too. The 1986 Motor Show, in the shadow of deregulation, marked the retreat of the bus and coach display to a cameo appearance in The Forum. It was the end of the era where the whole UK motor industry featured in a single show. The car park shuttles that year were provided by Midland Red North using mainly high-floor coaches together with the previously noted MAN artics and hired-in vehicles from smaller operators in their area including Chase Coaches.

Regular bus services bringing visitors to the NEC have always served Birmingham International Station on the western side of the complex. In the NEC's ten years prior to deregulation, the prime service was WMPTE's 159, the former Midland Red Birmingham to Coventry service.

This photographic survey illustrates a selection of the vehicles involved over those first ten years with particular focus on the support for the Motor Shows in 1978, 1982 and 1986. ∎

TOP LEFT: **Alongside the Maglev fixed link between the NEC (Birmingham International Station) and Birmingham Airport, a shuttle bus service was provided using one of the former NEC car park service Leyland Nationals. WMPTE 4791 (KOM 791P) awaits custom at the station during the 1984 Motor Show. In the background a local Austin Rover dealer is displaying a Mini Metro.**

TOP RIGHT: **Midland Red East adopted a darker shade of red soon after its formation in September 1981, applying it to a batch of former London Transport DMS-type Daimler Fleetlines. During the 1982 Motor Show, two are seen above the M42 at junction 6 heading back to the NEC to await the evening exodus. On hire to Midland Red Express labels are carried.**

MIDDLE: **Midland Red North also contributed double-deckers to the 1982 park-and-ride operation, supplying both former Harper Brothers vehicles and some indigenous to Midland Red such as Daimler Fleetline 6191 (UHA 191H). The external car parks were given animal references and 6191 has a distinctive elephant pictogram in the windscreen.**

LEFT: **Among the assorted Fleetlines hired for the 1982 Motor Show were these two 1981 Leyland-engined Bristol VRTs from PMT. The lead vehicle, 713 (NEH 731W), was withdrawn in 2002 and sold for preservation.**

ABOVE: **Midland Red Express received the batch of Willowbrook 003 bodied Leyland Leopards on order when the Midland Red company was split up in September 1981, the chassis having been built the previous year. They were used on Motor Show services in 1982 and most later passed to other Midland Red companies. Belying the fact that it is almost new, 839 (LOA 839X) loads for an external car park shuttle. It later joined the Midland Fox fleet.**

RIGHT: **On a very wet day during the 1986 Motor Show, Midland Red North 1508 (A508HVT), a Plaxton Paramount 3500 bodied Leyland Tiger finished with the blue Hotspur band for the Shrewsbury area, loads at NEC Piazza.**

LEFT: **Midland Red Express finished a number of coaches in more traditional Midland Red colours including Leyland Leopard 522 (NOE 614R). In February 1985 it is seen at the NEC awaiting guests for a BMW event.**

ABOVE: **Chase Coaches provided a number of vehicles to support the 1986 Motor Show car park shuttles. A357 KFD is a Plaxton Paramount 3200-bodied Ford R1115.**

BELOW: **WMPTE service 159 provided the main bus link to the NEC prior to deregulation. MCW Metrobus 2348 (LOA 348X) heads for Birmingham during the 1984 Motor Show.**

Under Badgerline ownership, Eastern National received 20 Dennis Darts with Plaxton Pointer bodies in 1994. On a quiet Sunday morning in the summer of 1995 a number are parked in Colchester Bus Station.

Eastern National's final years

Eastern National, based in Chelmsford, was the main bus operator in Essex. Geoff Mills illustrates some of its vehicles in the 1990s and 2000s prior to the widespread appearance of First's corporate livery.

Coincidentally Badgerline used a yellow and green livery, in shades not very different from those of Eastern National. Consequently this Badgerline Leyland National doesn't look out of place in Colchester in 1994. It had been transferred to Eastern National to boost the fleet to compete with Colchester Borough Transport.

The southern area of Eastern National was set up as a separate business by Badgerline in 1990, trading as Thamesway. An Alexander-bodied Leyland Tiger in Eastern National colours carries the Thamesway name.

BELOW: **Thamesway used yellow, initially with dark red relief which was later changed to purple, as shown on a Leyland National in Southend in 1998. The bus had been new to Eastern National in 1978.**

BELOW: **In 1997 Eastern National took delivery of 13 Dennis Lances with Northern Counties bodies, a relatively unusual combination although a small number were operated by neighbouring Eastern Counties. They were the last Lances built for UK operation. This one is seen when new.**

BELOW: **Like most NBC companies Eastern National operated ECW-bodied Leyland Olympians, this being one of 15 with Gardner engines delivered in 1986. The location is Colchester Bus Station on a grey December day in 1997.**

BELOW: **A few long-wheelbase coach-seated Olympians were supplied to NBC operators in the south-east of England, primarily for commuter services to London. This Leyland TL11-engined coach, with ECW body, was new to Eastern National in 1986. This view dates from 1998, shortly before the bus was withdrawn.**

There were a few large orders for the Leyland Lynx in the late 1980s, including one from Eastern National for 30 buses which were delivered in 1988. This bus, 1400 (E400 HWC), was the first. It was photographed in Southend in Thamesway ownership in 1999.

RIGHT & BELOW: In 1995 a batch of 19 Plaxton-bodied Volvo B10Ms was supplied to Thamesway for London services. When new they were in City Saver colours, as seen in the 1995 view of 601 in Southend. In 2001 sister coach 611 is in an attractive livery promoting London's Victoria Coach Station. The lettering on the side promotes "convenient connections to 1,000 destinations by coach".

BOTTOM RIGHT: Under First ownership this 1994 Yorkshire Rider Volvo Olympian was transferred south to Eastern National in 1998. It has a lowheight 76-seat Northern Counties body and is seen in Colchester in 2001.

In the 1960s and 1970s rear-engined buses were often viewed as unreliable. Tell that to this 26-year-old Bristol VRT, seen in Colchester in 2005 after being repainted in the colours used by Eastern National when the company was privatised. It has been preserved in this livery.

BELOW: To mark 75 years of Eastern National in 2004, this Alexander-bodied Dennis Dart was repainted in traditional style green and cream. The bus was new to Yorkshire Rider in 1995, joined Eastern National in 2000, and is seen outside Chelmsford Station in 2007.

Bremen by bus

Bob Hind samples public transport in a busy German city.

ABOVE: **An MAN artic heads east on route 24, picking up at Domsheide close to the River Weser.**

Like so many European cities Bremen, in Northern Germany, has a first-class tram system. Ten lines cross the city from north to south and east to west 20 hours a day. The fleet is comfortable, quiet, it glides effortlessly over the cobbled streets and the whole experience of travelling by tram is totally relaxed. Which is why on my second visit to this beautiful city I was determined to ignore the trams and try the bus network which, as much as it pains me to say, has obviously been designed to complement the tram system by filling in lots of gaps.

To be fair, that should not be seen as a criticism as together bus and tram provide a public transport network that any city would be proud of. Bremen is by no means a big city, with a population of 550,000; it straddles the River Weser on its final leg to the

port of Bremerhaven on the North Sea, and 332 buses and trams provide convenient, regular and generally very punctual services to every point of the urban areas and its surrounds.

Bremen Strassenbahn Aktiengesellschaft (BSAG) is the municipally-run company charged with moving the citizens of Bremen and their visitors safely around their city. BSAG's predecessors starting running horse-drawn trams in 1876 so there is some experience and heritage behind the professional face of the operator. Its 2000 employees (56 per cent of whom are drivers) provide eight tram lines and 44 bus lines with a fleet of 120 low-floor and 162 articulated buses and 50 conventional two-axle

ABOVE: **A splendid backcloth to the range of urban transport in Bremen.**

vehicles. The co-ordinated network carries 103 million passengers annually.

On-line, BSAG provides a very comprehensive schematic map showing bus, tram, regional bus and train lines. Timetables show a time at every stop served, and a range of fares options are available. On board the trams there are ticket vending machines and there are machines at principle locations but, on the buses, the driver will sell you a ticket although you will be in a very small minority. The vast majority of the Bremen travelling public pre-purchase from a range of multi-modal tickets and, I concluded, must be the most honest public transport users in Europe. On each vehicle there is a ticket validator (strangely, adjacent to the centre door) but I rarely saw it used. Most passengers board in the centre so never show the driver any sort of authentication and on my day trip I never saw any ticket checking. In fact at the bus drivers' entrance there is a barrier, which can presumably be activated to prevent fare-dodgers, but at busy times, when passengers boarded through every available door, they pushed past the barrier without any

RIGHT: **A Mercedes-Benz Citaro on service 26 at its northern terminus at Waller prepares to head south.**

consequence.

Hard copy pocket-sized timetable leaflets are available from the company's offices at the main railway station and in the old town at Domsheide adjacent to the cathedral. This was where I bought my day ticket in preparation for my excursion on BSAG buses; at €7.10 it wasn't cheap but I think I got my money's worth and it did give bus and tram travel within the greater city area which covered the whole of Bremen and its environs.

"Clunk" and I had registered

Just about the whole network converges on Bremen's main railway station, the Hauptbahnhof. The imposing facade of the Deutsche Bahn station is approached across a wide-open apron where

people nonchalantly mingle with trams and buses and health and safety regulations seem completely unnecessary. In front of the railway station are three long platforms used by the local bus network and the interurban buses. Displays at the ends of the stands show which services depart from each stand, again trams and buses share, but the first thing I found is that it depends in which order your service arrives as to where you are able to board.

In consequence, my 0809 service 20 entered the empty stand and picked up at three different points as passengers appeared from all directions. I properly validated my very small day ticket that the office clerk had told me had to be folded in two to access the validator. A "clunk" told me I had registered. The 50-seater (86 standees) Mercedes Citaro artic set off at 0812 through peak-hour traffic and headed for office-land running parallel to the east side of the river where old harbour-side warehouses had been converted into smart new office blocks and light industrial units. Service 20 is half-hourly (hourly evenings and Sundays) which perhaps reflects that half of its route is through light industry before it disappears into the nearby

countryside.

Digital and audio displays informed me as we approached each stop so, with that assistance and my map, I could confidently enjoy the landscape. My 19-minute journey to Waller Ring, a tram intersection north-west of the city centre, was as far as the local bus network ran northwards. There is a smaller local bus network around Bremen-North but the link between the two can only be made by tram and one regional bus route.

My plan was to circumnavigate the outer Bremen suburbs clockwise; most bus routes are radial and cross-city so linking up at points around the periphery was a challenge, which, in the main, proved easier than I had anticipated. Bus stop information was also to the high standard I had already experienced: usually a network map and relevant timetables; I was even impressed by a temporary bus stop in the middle of some road works that had a full timetable attached to it.

Service 28 started from one stop before where I was waiting. It was half-hourly up to 1400 then doubled in frequency until the half-hourly evening service dropped finally to hourly. The slow start might have been something to do with the fact that its destination was the University. My bus, a 53-seater MAN with standing for 94, arrived promptly at 0844 and continued through pleasant cobbled residential streets. Gradually these gave way to growing countryside and a stop, at the easily translated Campingplatz, was situated next to a

LEFT: **Arrival at the bus, train and tram interchange at Mahndorf.**

large wooded lake which was obviously a convenient weekend retreat for the people of Bremen, just 15 minutes out of the city centre. The next stop summed it up - Stadtwaldsee, literally town, wood, lake. My German was improving by the mile or kilometre!

My interest in rural pursuits was brought to an abrupt end as we met a queue of traffic and crawled towards some traffic lights. There seemed to be no obstruction other than the volume of vehicles waiting to cross this junction. The consequence was, however, that we entered the University campus 6 minutes late so I was resigned to having missed my next connection. My frustration was further compounded when I left my 28 at the University terminus only to see it turn round to become the 21 I had intended catching. Needless to say the driver was unaware of my intentions and sailed by.

However the University is well-served by both tram and bus so an alternative, service 31, was soon available and eight minutes later, at 0922, I was on a Solaris-bodied Mercedes with a number of early-morning students for the short link to Horner Kirche. This is a small shopping centre and another interchange with the east-west tram line. Interestingly both bus and tram used the central reservation for passenger movements.

The circus and a Leicester tram
Services 33/34 would complete a large chunk of the trip round the east side of Bremen. Starting at Horner Kirche, the 0930 34 would take me round to Sebaldsbruck, the southern end of the trams but with an interesting little secret. 33/34 operate a combined 10 minute headway which halves into the evening and Sunday frequency; there is a route split midway.

As we left at 0931 we were soon fringing the countryside and I was surprised that such a frequent route was serving so many grand houses with stables. At Muhlenfeldstrasse, the Olympia Circus was awakening after the previous night's performance and at the level crossing at Bahnhof Oberneuland, the driver switched off his engine while we waited for a Deutsche Bahn freight train, which seemed endless. BSAG drivers are simply uniformed in white shirt and grey slacks and generally seemed quite laid-back whilst keeping to schedule. I had yet to see any cash handling so perhaps life as a Bremen bus driver was more relaxed than it is for their British counterparts.

The upmarket houses and green fields continued

ABOVE: **The beautiful architecturally-designed bus shelter at Huckelriede Interchange, with an MAN in the background.**

until we met the main road at Osterholzer Heerstrasse and turned back towards the city. Three stops later we turned into the bus station at Sebaldsbruck where tram lines 2 and 10 terminate at Das Depot, a former tram shed now the home of Friends of Bremen Tramways. To confirm the nostalgia, a preserved tram, identical to the one donated by Krefeld in the 1980s to its twin UK town, Leicester, appeared in the doorway. The gift from Krefeld was somewhat embarrassing and the tram spent some years in the Abbey Park Road depot waiting for a more suitable home. The vintage trams at Sebaldsbruck do venture out on service at weekends and holidays so the tram enthusiasts are well catered for.

The bus station at Sebaldsbruck was obviously a busy location; alongside the central entrance a large residence housed the local offices of BSAG and drivers wandered in and out of the facility. The numbers of passengers waiting for a range of services were probably influenced by the near-by Mercedes-Benz plant.

My next bus, at 1021 on route 37, headed back along the Ottersberg main road and then turned off into the leafy village of Am Siek that seemed to consist of low-rise flats and the German equivalent of council houses. Within 10 minutes we were in the bustling town of Schweizer Eck, the local shopping centre and market, where the 37 off-loaded the majority of its passengers. This half-hourly service runs throughout the week and only increases in frequency at Monday to Friday peak times. The route, through narrow tree-lined streets, but with smaller houses, suggested this was not one of the BSAG's most profitable, but still warranted seven-day operation.

The bisected bus station

At the furthest southern outskirts of Bremen, in Am Grossen Kuhkamp, we circled an island with bronze cattle at its centre then headed into open fields to the 37's terminal at Bahnhof Mahndorf. Here we not only met the end of the tram line 1 but also the regional railway. On arrival there seemed to be only two stops adjacent to the railway platform, for our bus and an outgoing tram. I was a little bewildered as to where I would find the rest of the bus routes which were supposed to terminate at this interchange when I realised that the railway track actually bisected the bus station and the remaining bus stops were on the other side across a steep railway bridge, which, at least, gave me an aerial view of the lay-out.

Services 40, 41 and 44 serve the south-east corner of the suburbs but also link the end of tram line 1 to the southern termini of tram lines 2, 3 and 10. Combined frequencies ranged from every 10 to every 30 minutes, again throughout the week and with a weekday service starting at 0418 and finishing at 0036. So I did not have to wait long for my 40, due at 1059, which departed 2 minutes later.

To prove we were still in the country suburbs, fields abutted the quiet roads although houses lined the city side and the Mercedes artic was surprisingly busy. As the surroundings became more built up, I left the bus three stops short of its terminus at Weserwehr, to join service 29 at Christernstrasse. The 29 had come from beyond the Mercedes plant at Sebaldsbruck, which I had left an hour earlier but was now only one stop away. This half-hourly route was a strange affair: at 1121 (a minute early) the artic left along a busy street, served two more stops and then entered the motorway for a 10-minute dash across the river before exiting, serving three more stops and arriving at the end of its route, at Kattenturm-Mitte promptly at 1136. Only it wasn't the end of the route. The driver immediately turned

the destination to service 52 to Huchting (the other end of tram line 1) via the airport and headed off. Looking at the two timetables later, I found that the 29/52 provided a continuous half-hourly route across the eastern suburbs, a round trip of 111 minutes with the 9 minutes recovery all taken at the 29 terminus. Very efficient.

Let down by a seven-minute link

The Kattenturm-Mitte stop was, again, adjacent to the tramway, this time lines 4 and 5. There was evidence of two other bus routes but no sign of the next bus I intended to catch. A busy local shopping centre was next to the tram line so I ventured in, in the hope that I might find some information as to the whereabouts of service 53. I only needed this bus for a short seven-minute link to my next connection so as I emerged from the shops, I was more than frustrated to find the stop on the other side of the centre and my bus leaving five minutes early.

Although the 53 ran every 20 minutes, providing a daily link to IKEA up to 2300 (is IKEA open that late?) in a fit of pique, I returned to the tram station knowing that the next tram 4 would get me to Huckelriede in half the time. It did and despite missing the 53, I was able to get the 1207 service 27 I had aimed for, which would return to the city centre. The terminus at Huckelriede, which was shared by two tram lines and four bus routes, was almost upmarket, art deco style with beautiful amber tinted glass shelters laid out on a very spacious concourse.

The 26/27 service provide a very frequent (every 7/8 minutes during the day, 20 evenings and Sundays) cross-city link which I thought I would try out but having tasted three quarters of the suburbs around Bremen, I was anxious to complete the fourth, north-west quarter which was semi-rural but with a large container base adjacent to the river. I am usually quite meticulous in my planning of these trips but on this occasion had not sourced the timetables that would take me into that area. I knew the principal route from the city centre, the 63, ran every 15 minutes and, having experienced a morning of decent, frequent, punctual services, thought I would take the small risk of venturing into the unknown.

This involved leaving the 27 at Pappelstrasse in the Alte Neustadt (old new town) area, which I did, at 1220, crossed a congested dual-carriageway and tram track and boarded the 63, three minutes later. Four stops later I alighted at a point where I thought I would find the service that would give me a circular route of the outlying area. It did, if I was prepared to wait eight hours as, for some reason I have yet to discover, this route only ran evenings and weekends. My fall-back option only ran hourly and the next one was not for another 50 minutes so, feeling lunchtime pangs, I decided to abandon this last experiment and head back to the city centre on the next 63.

ABOVE: **Welcome to Bremen. A Bristol Lodekka parked at Bremen Airport and used for advertising and hospitality. It was new in 1967 to Eastern Counties and later operated for Eastern Scottish.**

Trams, buses and pedestrians happily co-exist
After lunch, I did venture back to Georg-Henschel Strasse where BLG Logistics dominated the landscape and container lorries queued to enter the terminal. A little bizarrely, although there seemed to be nothing but container facilities for as far as I could see, my return journey discovered the village of Rablinghausen just six minutes away that could not have created a greater contrast to the activities of the shipping lines if it had tried. I returned to the Hauptbahnhof on service 24, another Solaris, which linked Rablinghausen with the city centre every 7/8 minutes. It followed the opposite bank of the River Weser that I had started along that morning but this time heavily residential as we neared the city. I arrived at the central station and bus station at 1658 and evening peak was in full swing. Trams, buses and pedestrians still co-existed without any apparent safety issues so I decided I would finish my day out with one last round trip which would take me circuitously back to the cathedral square where I was staying.

I had already experienced the highly-popular 26/27 routes on the other side of the river earlier that day, now I joined it for part of its northern leg at 1708 that, as we left the station, was near to its 136-passenger capacity. The route leaves the city alongside the Burgerpark but that burst of greenery soon gives way to the German equivalent of terraced streets. I left

the 26 at Hemmstrasse where I had hoped to catch a 25, which would circle the north side of the city centre and re-enter from the west to Domsheide, next to the cathedral.

The 25 is another high frequency route, every 7/8 during the daytime, so I had no qualms about connections. However when I had alighted from the 26 and crossed the road to the 25 stop, I managed to glean, by rough translation, that the stop was out of commission and the service had been re-routed and would pick up round the corner. Round the corner I found a digital display showing the time of the next 25 and a couple of waiting passengers who joined my bewilderment when the 25 sailed by. There appeared to be more activity at a stop further up the road so we all decided that might be a better option. At 1734 (on time) my final Solaris of the day did pick us up and we completed the inner city circle in 14 minutes.

Despite a couple of hiccups, I enjoyed my tour of Bremen and was quite impressed by the levels and quality of service. I am still pinching myself on the issue of German honesty but perhaps I am wrongly judging the residents of Bremen. I am not a great tram lover but the integration of bus and tram produces a very effective and comprehensive network here and passenger loadings seem to confirm that BSAG have got it right. Sometimes I wonder what home would have been like if we had not been so quick to dismantle tram and trolley lines after the war. We might have been truly continental. ∎

Barnsley buses

Barnsley bustles with buses. **John Young** illustrates a selection of recent vehicles, starting in the town centre then working out to its hinterland.

Most of the buses in this batch have now become training vehicles, but this Stagecoach Alexander ALX300-bodied MAN is seen setting out from Barnsley on the long run to Doncaster via Wombwell, Wath, Mexborough and Conisbrough.

RIGHT: **A view of Barnsley Interchange taken from the multi-storey car park that is due for demolition as part of the town centre redevelopment. In the foreground is a Stagecoach ADL Enviro200. Also visible are a Townlines-branded Stagecoach MAN, a pair of Red Line buses and a class 144 diesel unit providing a Sheffield to Leeds service.**

BELOW: **Arriva Yorkshire operates an hourly service to Barnsley from Wakefield via Royston. A Wrightbus-bodied VDL SB200 approaches the Interchange on Eldon Street.**

ABOVE: **Stagecoach Yorkshire added 14 of the new ADL Enviro200 MMCs to its fleet in early 2016. All can be seen in Barnsley, with four used on local route 11 to Athersley North and the other ten on the 22X to Rotherham via Wath. The 22X buses work out of Rawmarsh depot. Both batches are route-branded; a 22X is shown here.**

ABOVE: **A standard Stagecoach ADL Enviro200 works a journey on the Hospital and Darton corridor past the Town Hall and the piece of modern art known locally as "the nit comb".**

ABOVE: **While under the short-lived influence of Island Fortitude, Tate's received four King Long service buses. One of the pair of short examples sets out on commercial service X10 to Meadowhall via Chapeltown, a service that was withdrawn before the business failed in February 2016.**

ABOVE: **Services on the busy Pontefract Road corridor provide a combined five-minute daytime headway, with long-distance services from Pontefract coordinated with more local offerings from Grimethorpe and Cudworth. Eight of the relatively-rare East Lancs Kinetic-bodied MANs were transferred to Yorkshire from Stagecoach Scotland. One is seen outside the Star public house in Cudworth on service 29 from Upton via Hemsworth in the spring of 2016.**

RIGHT: **Red Line Buses went out of business in May 2014. The fleet mainly comprised Darts and Solos but also included this Plaxton Primo, seen at Hoyle Mill. It is neither red nor does it feature a line. Operations covered several key routes, but with low frequencies, irregular timetables and poor punctuality. Scheduled operations had finished for the day before the evening peak concluded.**

ABOVE: **This Stagecoach oddity was new to 2 Travel in South Wales but joined the group by way of Duke's of Coleford in 2006. The MCV Stirling-bodied MAN is passing Cudworth bridge on a service 28 journey from Pontefract. The bridge, which carried a disused railway line, has since been removed to allow double-deckers to serve the area.**

TOP RIGHT: **Waterson's was a small coach operator based in Hemsworth, West Yorkshire, who stepped in to fill perceived gaps in the market following the demise of Red Line. Scanias are favoured for bus work with operations centred on the Grimethorpe area. This L94UB has a Wrightbus Solar body and was originally a two-door bus with APCOA, the airport car park operator.**

MIDDLE: **Stagecoach service 217 passes through three local authority areas - Rotherham, Doncaster and Barnsley. Shortly after heavy rain, a Dennis Dart approaches Adwick-upon-Dearne bound for Thurnscoe.**

BELOW: **Until May 2015, when it was truncated at Wath, First operated a competing service from Rotherham through the Dearne Valley to Barnsley. Initially using youthful route-branded single-deckers, operations moved over to predominantly older double-deckers. A Volvo B7TL passes under the railway bridge at Doncaster Road, Stairfoot, on the outskirts of Barnsley.**

BELOW: **Stagecoach Yorkshire operates 37 Scania ADL Enviro400s, shared between Chesterfield and Ecclesfield depots. The latter provides service 265, a trunk route from Barnsley to Sheffield via Chapeltown. Here it passes through the idyllic setting of Worsbrough Village.**

There are two Volvo B7TLs with East Lancs Vyking bodywork still in the Stagecoach fleet that originated with the Yorkshire Traction business. One of them was chosen to carry heritage livery to mark the tenth anniversary of Stagecoach in Barnsley. The move was well received by customers and staff alike. Service 66 is the most significant double-deck service in Barnsley, running every ten minutes to Birdwell, Hoyland and Elsecar.

BELOW: **When Tate's ceased operations suddenly in February 2016 Stagecoach stepped in with immediate effect to replace a number of routes. One of the contracted services running out to Penistone is service 92, seen here being run by an MAN at Hoylandswaine.**

ABOVE: **Eleven East Lancs-bodied MANs were purchased by Yorkshire Traction. Known as Penistone MANs by virtue of their purchase as part of a Kickstart scheme to reinvigorate services in the area, the last examples left the fleet in 2016. One leaves Holmfirth for Barnsley in August 2009 on a journey that will take it over stunning Pennine moorland to Penistone and eventually to more urban surroundings. This route was subsequently split at Penistone with the Holmfirth leg won on tender by Tate's. When they ceased operations in February 2016, Stagecoach regained the work, but now uses Optare Solos.**

Exploring Guernsey – it's better by bus.

A week's holiday in the of summer 2015 gave **David Jukes** the ideal opportunity to revisit a Channel Island last seen as a teenager almost 30 years earlier.

All photographs by the author.

ABOVE: **Passing the North Plantation in St Peter Port in August 2015 is CT Plus DM14 (70025), an East Lancs Myllennium-bodied Dennis Dart SLF new in March 2003 as Island Coachways 25.**

The island of Guernsey is located within the Gulf of St Malo off the north-west French coast. It is a dependency of the Crown that forms part of the British Isles but not the United Kingdom. As such, Guernsey enjoys full independence although international relations and the island's defence are in the British government's hands.

Responsibility for the island's scheduled bus services rests with the States of Guernsey Environment Department in conjunction with the contracted operator – since 1 April 2012, the HCT Group's CT Plus Guernsey subsidiary.

The dominant bus operators for many years were the Guernsey Railway Company and Guernsey Motors. Many independent operators were acquired by either undertaking over a number of years until the last, Watson's Greys of St Martin, sold out in 1978.

Both operators were owned by the United Transport group from 1950 until sale to William Allen Smith in 1975 before passing to Steiner Investments in 1979. The business closed on 19 November 1980 with little notice given, leaving Guernsey without a proper bus service for 89 days. Trafalgar Leisure International's tender was accepted by the island authorities and Guernseybus started limited services on 16 February 1981 with full provision following a week later.

Another CT Plus ex-Island Coachways Dart, DM4 (70015), splashes away from the St Peter Port bus terminus in South Esplanade.

Financial struggles in 1995 caused by declining passenger numbers led the sharing of bus operations with Island Coachways. The Passenger Transport Licensing Authority contracted Guernseybus to run 11 routes and Island Coachways four. Guernseybus ceased operations on 28 November 2000; Island Coachways took over its routes from the following day. A new network was designed by Southern Vectis for operation by Island Coachways – this took effect on 12 March 2001.

The States of Guernsey acquired 33 new low-floor East Lancs Myllennium-bodied Dennis Dart SLFs for operation by Island Coachways. These were 2.35metres wide and 9.67metres long (Island legislation permits maximums of 2.49metres and 9.75metres respectively) and delivered between

December 2002 and May 2003 as Island Coachways 12-44, registered 70012-44.

The new buses were followed by eight further low-floor Dennis Dart SLFs in 2008/09. These Caetano Nimbus-bodied buses date from 2004/05 and were also built to the narrow 2.35metres width but to a shorter 8.8metres length. The new arrivals were numbered 11, 55/6, 66, 77, 88, 91/9 by Island Coachways to match their new 700xx registrations.

All 33 have been operated by CT Plus Guernsey since April 2012; the East Lancs-bodied examples as DM1-33 and the Caetano-

RIGHT: Also leaving St Peter Port bus is CT Plus-operated DCS15 (70088), a Caetano Nimbus-bodied Dennis Dart SLF new to East Midlands Airport Car Parks in April 2005 as 6 (FJ05 HYK). It was operated by Island Coachways between July 2008 and March 2012.

ABOVE: **There is little apparent difference in size between Intransit 1787, a 1954 ex-Watson's Reading-bodied Albion Victor FT39AN, and Island Coachways 5779, a Plaxton Cheetah-bodied Mercedes-Benz O814D new to the operator in February 2007. The Albion seats 36 and the Mercedes 29.**

bodied buses as DCS10-17 – all in registration order (DCS1-9 are Caetano-bodied Dennis Darts within the CT Plus London fleet).

The previous operator's green and yellow livery is maintained – most, if not all of the East Lancs-bodied fleet retain their original application with references to Island Coachways carefully removed. Fading paint is noticeable when a more recently-painted Caetano-bodied Dart is positioned alongside or where paintwork has been touched up. Overall advertising liveries are carried by a handful of buses; the shorter Darts are preferred for this treatment.

The majority of bus fares in the of summer 2015 were fixed at £1 per journey regardless of length - a trip on the Guernsey Vaeux routes 91 and 92 around the island coast proved an absolute bargain. Exceptions were the late-night services from 10pm onwards which required a £2 cash fare per journey.

One-, two- or seven-day passes for individuals and families were also available, as were pre-paid bulk-discount tickets – we acquired 20

for £17 thereby paying 85p per journey. Free travel was available only to older residents of Guernsey, Alderney and Herm – visiting seniors had to pay the same fares as their younger fellow passengers.

Bus stops are either painted on the roads or indicated by conventional post-mounted signs – the former is most common outside of St Peter Port and St Sampson. Audible bus stop announcement equipment is not fitted to Guernsey's buses but we, like many island visitors, found it best to ask the driver when boarding to advise our required intermediate stop.

The buses themselves were clean; a ban on the consumption of food and drink on board and the fitting of CCTV surveillance no doubt assists. Seat spacing is a little tight in places, particularly in the raised rear section (most noticeably to your long-legged writer), but those in the know made for the rear seat next to the emergency exit where ample legroom existed.

More recently, State funding was granted in October 2015 to replace 12 buses with the remainder to be refurbished by CT Plus before their phased replacement by 2020. It will interesting to see what vehicles are acquired as the longer Darts are considered by many to be too large for the island's roads.

Appearing on island tours, private hires, hotel

LEFT: **Approaching journey's end at South Esplanade, St Peter Port, during Easter 1986 is Guernseybus 110 (21902), a 1969 Reading-bodied Bedford J4 new to Guernsey Motors. It was acquired by Guernseybus in 1981.**

transfers and suchlike were the mix of mini and midi-coaches operated by Island Coachways, Intransit Passenger Services and Island Taxis; these range in size from 16 to 43 seats.

Intransit also operates vintage tours using a 1954 former Watson's Reading-bodied Albion Victor FT39AN registered 1787. Undergoing restoration within the company's workshops is former Guernsey Motors 78 (8228), a 1959 Reading-bodied Albion Victor FT39KAN.

By way of a contrast, the Guernseybus fleet during your writer's previous visit at Easter 1986 consisted of a changing Bedford and Bristol mix. Older Bedfords were the surviving ex-Guernsey Railway Co and Guernsey Motors J4s, delivered between 1966 and 1974 with bodies by Reading, Sparshatt or Pennine Coachcraft. The Reading and Sparshatt examples perpetuated the J A Davis coach-outline body design that first appeared on Albion Victor chassis in 1950 and was somewhat outdated when specified for the operators' 1960s and 1970s deliveries. Newer Bedfords were ten Wadham Stringer-bodied Bedford SB5s delivered in two batches of five in 1976 and 1978; these and the J4s were built to Guernsey's then-maximum 7ft 4ins width, signified by Guernseybus applying an A prefix to their fleetnumbers.

The older Bristols were the four survivors of the 16 bus and six coach Eastern Coach Works-bodied Bristol SUL4As acquired by the Guernsey Railway Co in 1979/80 – these were

new to the Western and Southern National companies in the 1960s and replaced the island's remaining Albion Victors.

These were joined by a host of second-hand Bristol LH and LHS buses and coaches – a dozen ex-London Transport LH buses with ECW bodywork, one former London Country LHS bus also bodied by ECW, four ex-Western National and Devon General Marshall-bodied LHS buses and ten Plaxton Elite III-bodied LH coaches from Western National. More LH and LHS types were to follow in subsequent years.

Most of the Guernseybus fleet was painted plain white with the exceptions – Bedford J4 and Bristol LH and LHS – carrying overall advertising liveries of varying hues. These disappeared from the island's buses in the 1990s before making a comeback in 2009.

The photographs accompanying this feature were taken in August 2015, or at Easter 1986 to illustrate a previous generation of Guernsey's buses. ■

BELOW: **Seen in the Grand Bouet depot in 1986 are five second-hand members of the Guernseybus fleet. From left to right are 168 (31919), a 1975 Plaxton Elite III-bodied Bristol LH6L new to Greenslades; numbers 70, 68 and 65 (31929, 31927, 31924), 1976/77 Eastern Coach Works-bodied Bristol LH6Ls new to London Transport: and 74 (12728), a 1972 Marshall-bodied Bristol LHS6L new to Western National. All were acquired by Guernseybus in 1984/85.**

Not in the usual service

When buses reach the end of their service life not all end up in the scrapyard.
Tony Wilson illustrates some imaginative new uses for old buses.

ABOVE: **First up is this former Devon General Metro-Cammell-bodied AEC Regent V that by September 1976 had taken Holy Orders and been acquired by the Hounslow Evangelical Church in West London. The vehicle still bore the livery of the National Bus Company.**

RIGHT: **From Holy Orders to 'ello, 'ello 'ello, what do we have 'ere. This Eastern Coachworks-bodied Bristol FLF found alternative employment with the local constabulary in Bristol. By August 1978 it had been sold off by NBC's Bristol Omnibus subsidiary and put to good use as a mobile Crime Prevention vehicle.**

ABOVE: **AEC Regal RF 594 was originally based at London Transport's Windsor garage and was a regular performer on the long cross-London Green Line route 718 between Windsor and Epping. In 1973 it became a recruitment vehicle for London Country Bus Services, and is seen here in May 1976 at Northfleet garage. The promotional message was pretty bold - and gender specific.**

ABOVE: **Down to the West Country in Western National territory during July 1978. Helston bus garage at that time played host to mobile training unit TU6, a Bristol LS5G previously numbered 1684. It looked a bit forlorn and was also used by associated operators Devon General and Greenslades. It had been converted in 1970, and eight years later bears no obvious signs of corporate NBC branding.**

BELOW: **There were 838 AEC Swifts built for London Transport between 1969 and 1972, with Marshall, Metro-Cammell and Park Royal bodywork. By the early 1980s the fleet had all but completed their life in revenue-earning service in London. One or two managed to struggle on in other forms. One such vehicle was SMS 91 that ended front-line service in 1976 and was later converted into a mobile video service for London Buses and renumbered STB 91. It is seen on the airfield at the annual North Weald event in June 1986.**

BELOW: **The pupils of St Joseph's School for Boys situated in the North Kent town of Orpington in the 1970s were lucky enough to have their own transport. This former Lancashire United Transport vehicle had by June 1976 become the official transport for the school. The fine curved Plaxton body and AEC Reliance mechanics, contrasted with one of the more angular London Daimler Fleetlines on the north side of Hyde Park Corner. It appeared to retain the dual-purpose seating with which it was supplied to LUT in 1963.**

LEFT: **Now, are you sitting comfortably? Well, if not, this former Ipswich Borough Transport Optare Delta may have the answer. Converted into a mobile display for the Carer Collection of reclining and easier-sitting armchairs, the bus sat near a furniture shop displaying its wares instead of fares in Chesterfield during April 2004.**

ABOVE: **A Show Bus at Showbus. By a quirk of fate the South Yorkshire PTE had decided to promote its services with this Van Hool McArdle-bodied Ailsa B55 that bore the legend 'Show Bus' on the front and side panelling. It is seen at Showbus at Woburn Abbey in 1986. As well as changes to the interior, the nearside featured a large awning fitted between the decks to protect visitors - especially on sunny days at Woburn.**

TOP RIGHT: **Whilst still in the employ of London Buses during the late 1990s Daimler Fleetline DMS1515 was converted to promote the validity of the Travelcard and was dubbed as Supercar. These were the three elements of London bus, the London Underground and trains within the London Network Rail area. The feature at the rear was just an open shell.**

ABOVE RIGHT: **Something to put a smile on your face - or not, as the case may be. Bit of a come-down from the hard revenue-earning service of its earlier years with the Greater Glasgow PTE, but by 1992 this Leyland National had been trans-formed into a promotional tool for Strathclyde Buses.**

RIGHT: **A mobile office was what this full-fronted ECW-bodied Bristol SC had become, when con-verted by the Lincolnshire Road Car Company NBC subsidiary. It had at some stage been used as a left-luggage office at Skegness. Here it made an entrance to the June 1978 Showbus Rally held that year as part of the Hillingdon Country Show in West London**

BOTTOM RIGHT: **After the end of its front-line revenue-earning service this former West York-shire PTE Leyland Atlantean found a quite differ-ent employment. By January 1995 it had ventured away from its Northern roots (or should that be routes), southwards to rest alongside the M25 Motorway at South Mimms services on the north side of London. Here it was in use as a passen-ger and staff point for co-ordinated changeovers between touring coaches operated by Wallace Arnold.**

ABOVE: **This Leyland National, still owned by the Western National, transferred travellers from the railway station just over a mile through Weymouth to the Sealink Channel Island ferries terminal, complete with a trailer to transport the large quantities of luggage. It is seen in August 1981, with its destination reading Channel Islands.**

BELOW: **In the early 1980s this rather strange looking pseudo charabanc made an appearance in the south. Created on a 1973 Bristol LH6L chassis, the original ECW bodywork had been removed and replaced as shown. The bus was used for promotional work and also on various tourist routes in the Bournemouth and Poole area. It had originally been registered NLJ 516M and supplied to the Hants & Dorset company. It later moved north and subsequently received a pseudo Midland Red livery.**

When a Leyland Leopard in the associated Whites fleet of Chesterfield Transport came to mechanical grief in 1994, help was at hand. The bus had failed on a road in the Derbyshire Peak District that led up to the village of Eyam. Fortunately rescue came in the shape of the Chesterfield's wrecker. This was a converted Leyland Leopard with Duple coach body, originally supplied to Cumberland Motor Services.

ABOVE: **Publicity is an important tool for any organisation and with bus companies it comes in the shape of thousands of bus stops and other outlets, which require updating with information. In the Milton Keynes area during the early 2000s, Stagecoach made use of an Alexander-bodied Mercedes-Benz converted into a mobile publicity vehicle.**

BELOW: **Appearances can be deceiving and what one might think was a former bus is not always so. For instance this East Lancs Spryte-bodied Dennis Dart was produced as a mobile library for Durham County Council. In August 2002 the vehicle was on duty adjacent to the Tourist Information Office at Stanhope in Weardale. After several years the library was made redundant and it later became a church-based outreach vehicle in Derbyshire.**

ABOVE: **Various BBC Radio stations up and down the country acquired bus-based vehicles for outside broadcasting. Radio Cumbria used this East Lancs Myllennium-bodied MAN 14.220, the vehicle quite some way away from its local haunts when it visited the museum complex at RAF Cosford in Shropshire during 2008. A small note on the front bumper indicated that Scottish-based Keillor Coachbuilders had been instrumental in equipping the vehicle..**

BELOW: **And, finally, a bus created from something quite different. In the late 1990s the village of Polperro in Cornwall became the battleground of a mini bus war between two rival operations. The village with its narrow streets restricted motor vehicles, so more environmentally-friendly methods were necessary to transport visitors from the car park at the top of the village down to the harbour area. Whilst one operator relied on real horse-power another local entrepreneur acquired several converted electric-powered milk floats.**

An A to Z of bus brands

In a competitive business environment companies need to be noticed.
Graeme Palmer takes a look at bus company branding.

All photographs by the author.

ABOVE: **While the Arrows name has featured in other locations, it is perhaps most relevant in Hastings, where it provides an association with the town's infamous battle of 1066. This is a Stagecoach ADL Enviro200 in the summer of 2015.**

Many operators in the bus industry are big on branding. Whilst the majority of this is based on route numbers, many operators go down the route of the brand name. In this article, I shall give you an A to Z of sample brand names past and present – yes, it actually is possible to complete the entire alphabet with branding! By no means is this a definitive list, but it covers most of Britain.

First off, then, **A** is for Airlink – one the most popular brand names of all, with it having enjoyed use at Lothian, First Doncaster, First Glasgow, Arriva Manchester and Arriva Merseyside. It's also used in Ireland by Dublin Bus. A slight variation sees Airline used in Oxford. One of Go North East's best-known brands is the popular Angel. I've always considered Activ8 to be a clever brand; it's a joint effort by Stagecoach South and Go South Coast running between Salisbury and Andover. Meanwhile, Stagecoach South East is fond of its Arrows, having fired them around Hastings, Folkstone and Canterbury, past or present. Many will argue that

the A1 Service name which was used by Stagecoach Western was not a brand, but I felt it best to mention this too because of its popularity among enthusiasts.

B is for Blaydon Racers – one of several locally-inspired names used by Go North East. Keeping with the local inspiration, Go North East has also used Black Cats – a reference to Sunderland Association Football Club. One of TrentBarton's best known brands is the Black Cat, once a joint operation with independent operator Felix. Stagecoach also contribute to the B selection, with Buchan Xpress (formerly Buchan Link) in Aberdeenshire, Bassetlaw Belles in the East Midlands and Breeze in Kent. The Buchan Xpress and Breeze were both recipients of high-profile new buses in 2016. Breeze is also used by Stephenson's of Essex in Bury St Edmunds. B is for Busway too, a major brand name

LEFT: **Cardiff Bus is one of a dwindling number of UK operators to still use articulated buses. Some of these wear Baycar livery for the short service from the city centre to the regenerated Cardiff Bay, as seen in July 2012.**

Lancashire service 68. Coaster is another, being used by Brighton & Hove, Go North East and Stagecoach Western (as Clyde Coaster). Stagecoach Strathtay and Stagecoach Bluebird use a nice typical Stagecoach variation, Coastrider. And in Grimsby, Coastal Cruiser is used. Meanwhile, Coasthopper is an award-winning brand used in Norfolk. The name has also been used historically by Stagecoach Devon in Exmouth. One of Stagecoach's early brands was Citi, launched in Cambridge and subsequently rolled out in Peterborough. It has also seen use in Preston, Carlisle and Gloucester. Many Oxford Bus Company routes are now branded as "city". Meanwhile, Go North East uses Citylink and some Arriva routes in Leicester are branded as City Linx. In 2016 Transdev launched a new express route between York and Leeds, branded as City Zap. And in Southampton, First has introduced City Red, although it could well be argued this is a fleetname rather than a brand. Cardiff Bus, meanwhile, uses the names "Capital City Red" and "Capital City Green". Other brand names beginning with C that are worthy of mention are the Chesterfield Chief, the Chesterfield Chef, the Castle Line (also Chesterfield-based) and Culm Valley Connect at Stagecoach Devon. Finally for C, Circuit in Chichester is a clever variation on the names used for circular routes.

ABOVE: **Brighton & Hove's Coaster service was upgraded with Wrightbus Streetdecks in 2015. One is seen on Terminus Road in Eastbourne in July of that year.**

in Cambridgeshire with Stagecoach and Whippet. Finally, Cardiff Bus uses the name Baycar for its flagship service to Cardiff Bay.

C, in various forms, stands for city and coast. Coastliner is the most common coast-based name, seeing use with Arriva North East (306/308), Stagecoach South (700) and Arriva Cymru (as Cymru Coastliner). It was once used for Stagecoach's

D is definitely for Diamond. This name is used in Kent for routes linking Sandwich, Deal and Dover with Canterbury. Diamond is also a name used by Go North East. A curious coastal-based name used by Go North East is Drifter. Stagecoach North East is a recent convert to brand names, and now runs several routes in South Shields and Stockton as Dots – as in the phrase connecting the dots. In South Yorkshire, meanwhile, Dearne Link is another notable D.

E is a letter I struggled with a little, with the various Express options feeling rather predictable and prosaic. A clever recently-introduced name in Inverness, however, is ElectriCITY – used on electric-powered Solos operated by Stagecoach. Express City Connect, meanwhile, is a name used by

LEFT: **First's lengthy X1 Excel is operated by high-specification ADL Enviro400s, as seen in Peterborough's Queensgate Bus Station.**

LEFT: **Stagecoach's Perth service 7 was one of the original Gold services, originally branded as Goldline. The service is now on its second generation of vehicles, ADL Enviro300H hybrids. This photo was taken on South Street in April 2014.**

Durham. Arriva's Yorkshire Tiger uses Flying Tiger for airport routes. Centrebus uses the clever Five Counties name for its Nottingham to Peterborough route which runs through Nottinghamshire, Leicestershire, Rutland, Lincolnshire and Cambridgeshire. Flash has been applied to a number of routes by Plymouth Citybus, denoting higher specification vehicles with yellow, red, blue and green themes. Another recent introduction is Stagecoach South West's Falcon intercity express between Plymouth and Bristol.

G almost inevitably stands for Gold, with the number of places this Stagecoach brand appears being too numerous to list. Stagecoach wasn't the first to use gold though, for Gold Service was a quality branding used by First Manchester from the late 1990s. Go2 is a highly-successful network operated by Nottingham City Transport. Go2 has also seen use with Stagecoach in Devon. And a discussion of brands beginning with G would not be complete without the mention of one of Britain's oldest brands – Green Line, which continues to feature on coach services in Berkshire, Hertfordshire, Bedfordshire and Essex.

Stagecoach Fife. In Hampshire, Eclipse is the name for services on the Fareham to Gosport bus link. And in East Anglia, First brands its trunk X1 route from Lowestoft to Norwich as Excel.

F is a popular letter for various busways and bus-only routes. In Crawley, Fastway is used by Metrobus, while in Kent, Arriva Kent Thameside go with Fastrack. A more recent variation of the theme sees Fastlink being used by Stagecoach Glasgow. One of my favourite brands is Go North East's Fab Fifty Six. Elsewhere, ftr was used by First for its Wrightbus Streetcars in York, Leeds and Swansea. In Hull, Stagecoach has used the network brand Frequento. Arriva North East is using the similar name Frequenta in Darlington, Stockton and

H is for Humber FastCat, used on a joint service run by Stagecoach East Midlands and East Yorkshire Motor Services. In Leeds and Bradford, Hyperlink was until very recently used by First. Heart has seen

BELOW: **Ten hydrogen-powered H2-branded Van Hool buses operate in Aberdeen – four with First and six with Stagecoach. First's can be found on some workings of the X40 service, as seen on King Street in April 2016.**

BELOW: **The Jet name is used on Stagecoach services to airports across Scotland, including the 747 which links Edinburgh Airport with park-and-ride sites in Fife.**

RIGHT: **Shown here is the network Lakes Connection livery for Stagecoach services in the Lake District. This is Ambleside, during typically inclement weather in the summer of 2014.**

use with Stagecoach in Carlisle, and in Folkstone and Dover. Hop, meanwhile, is used by Stagecoach in Canterbury and on Devon services 11 and 12. Also, on Aberdeen's flagship hydrogen bus project the Van Hool vehicles are branded as H2 Aberdeen.

I is for InterConnect, an award-winning interurban network in Lincolnshire, mostly run by Stagecoach. Indigo is the name for the TrentBarton service formerly known as Rainbow 5, while i4 is the present name for the former Rainbow 4. Indigo is also used by Go North East, bizarrely with pink buses.

J is for Jet, an airport service brand name used by Stagecoach in Orkney, Inverness, Aberdeen and Fife. Stagecoach South uses the Jazz name for services in Basingstoke. Another award-winning brand worthy of mention is the Jurassic Coaster used by First Dorset for its service X53.

K is another letter I really struggled with. Stagecoach's Kite brand in Surrey was the only current one I could think of. Going quite a bit further back, in the 1980s and 1990s employee-owned Busways and later Stagecoach Busways used the Killingworth Express name for direct routes to the town.

L is for Loop – a popular name for urban circular

BELOW: **The use of the Platinum brand by First is restricted to Aberdeen, where three routes now use the name. Service 13 was the third route to convert and the first to do so with new vehicles, as illustrated by an ADL Enviro200 MMC at the Seaton terminus of the route in April 2016.**

services, seeing use with Stagecoach in Thanet, Eastbourne and historically in Elgin. It is also used in Gateshead by Go North East. In the 1990s and early 2000s, various Stagecoach routes in the Lake District were branded as Lakeland Experience. Today, the name has evolved to Lakes Connection. Other noteworthy L names are Go North East's Lambton Worm (another name derived from local culture) and the Lynx brand used by Stagecoach in Worksop for Robin Hood Airport services. Local Linx, meanwhile, appears on Arriva vehicles in Leicester. Reading Buses has started to move to brand names. Most of these orientate around the names of colours, but routes to Wokingham and Bracknell are respectively branded as Leopard and Lion.

M has three iconic brand names. The longest-used

BELOW: **Go North East's Quaylink service is now operated commercially. Illustrating the purple version of the latest livery is an Optare Versa, seen at Fewster Square in April 2016.**

ABOVE: **Arriva's premium Sapphire brand can be found far and wide, with a recent convert being the 100/101/102 services that link Stevenage with Hitchin and Luton. It is operated by VDL SB200s cascaded from Merseyside; one is seen at Stevenage Bus Station.**

is Magic Bus, a name now found just in Manchester, but historically it has surfaced in Newcastle, Liverpool, Glasgow, Ayr and Irvine (as Magic Mini). Another award-winning name is Go South Coast's More, originally used for services linking Poole, Bournemouth and Christchurch. More is now the fleetname for the company's Dorset network. Obviously the letter M couldn't be passed by without mention of Arriva's MAX brand, which started off as a North East and Yorkshire initiative but has since been rolled out in other fleets. Beyond those, Mainline is the name used in Burnley for Transdev's trunk route linking the town with Padiham, Nelson and Colne before branching out to other significant destinations including major towns like Accrington, Clitheroe, Skipton and Keighley. Arriva uses the similar Medway Mainline name as a network brand. Metrolink is the name for free city centre routes in Manchester, operated by First. Finally, M is a common letter for branding in Mansfield, with Mansfield Move and Mansfield Miller both being used in the Nottinghamshire town.

N is a surprisingly challenging letter, but is represented by Stagecoach Devon's North Devon Wave. Until recently, N was used by Go North East on North Tyne Links services, which are now branded as Indigo. N also stands for New Forest Tour, used by Go South Coast, while First Aberdeen brands one of its city routes as Northern Lights.

O is for Oxford Tube – a long-established name that Stagecoach inherited from Transit Holdings. Another long-standing name beginning with O is, of course,

Birmingham's famous Outer Circle service 11A/C. In the last years of municipal ownership, Blackburn Transport branded its outer circle route as The O/C in a striking purple and orange livery. Continuing the circular theme, O also stands for Orbit, a name historically used by both Go North East and Preston Bus.

It would be lazy of me to say **P** is for Park & Ride, but wrong not to mention what is easily the most widely-used brand name. P is for Platinum, used for premium-specification routes by First Aberdeen and National Express West Midlands. Pulse is a popular name, used by Stagecoach South in Worthing, as a network brand by First Leeds, and historically also used by Go North East. Another historical brand for Go North East is Pronto, a name which is also used by TrentBarton and Stagecoach East Midlands. Also for P, I quite liked the old Popin brand used by Stagecoach in Swindon, which I felt was a clever play on words (as in "pop in to town").

Q is unsurprisingly a letter that offers little. However, it is used for one well-known service, the Quaylink in Newcastle and Gateshead, now operated commercially by Go North East but originally operated under contract to Nexus by Stagecoach with Designline vehicles which were unique in the UK. Q also stands for Quorum – Arriva until recently branded a few express services as Quorum Express, and continues to brand another route as Quorum Shuttle. They serve the Quorum Business Park in Newcastle-upon-Tyne.

R is for Rainbow One – I feel it would be wrong to represent the letter with anything but this significant TrentBarton brand. R also stands for red, and there is no shortage of red-inspired brands – Red Arrow (singular) at TrentBarton, Red Arrows (plural) and Red Kite at Go North East, and now Red Express with Transdev in Lancashire – bizarrely with a livery dominated by blue! Red Arrow features in London with services 507/521, albeit the name does not currently appear on vehicles, save for one bus in heritage livery. Red Rocket, meanwhile, is a former branding used by Go South Coast in Eastleigh. Beyond the red theme, R also stands for the Rivers brand used by Stagecoach South, for Regency at Brighton & Hove, and for First's RailAir service in Reading. Finally, First Borders now brands the lengthy X95 service between Edinburgh and Carlisle as The Ridings, a reference to the Common Ridings, an equestrian event staged in Scottish border towns.

S is quite a contested letter, but it would be amiss not to begin with Arriva's premium product, Sapphire. A favourite brand of many an enthusiast is the innovative and award winning Seasiders used by Stagecoach in Skegness. Simplicity is a network name used by First Glasgow, and also sees use in Sunderland with Go North East. S is definitely for Star. The most obvious use of the name is in Corby, but Stagecoach has also brought Stars to the streets of Andover, Bognor and Thanet. Star is also the current name for First services between Portsmouth and Waterlooville. Representing S in TrentBarton is Skylink, used for airport routes. Another name I quite like the thought behind is the now retired Sail branding used by Stagecoach in Portsmouth – an effective reference to Portsmouth's harbour economy. Finally for S, Stagecoach in Worksop uses the branding of Sherwood Arrow.

It is hard to choose a brand to lead with for the letter T, but I am going with Traws Cymru, which is used for various long-distance routes across Wales. TransPeak, meanwhile, is the long-established name of the trunk Peak District route between Derby, Buxton and Manchester now operated by High Peak. In Kent, Triangle has been used for services linking Canterbury with Herne Bay and Whitstable for 12 years now, with the third generation of Triangle-branded vehicles on the route arriving in 2016. Another well-established T is Townlines, used by Stagecoach in Barnsley. In Dundee, Stagecoach Strathtay brands its busiest route as Tayway (previously Travel Tayway), while the Stagecoach Fife service into the city is branded as Taylink. In Aberdeen, First has introduced colour-related brand names, with the Thistle Line being my personal favourite. When it was launched, Ten was quite a clever brand at Go North East, with service 10 running every 10 minutes with a fleet of 10 vehicles and a weekly ticket priced at £10. It perhaps doesn't work quite so well now that there are 13 vehicles and the weekly ticket is priced at a choice of £15.50 or £22.90. Another Go North East brand worthy of mentioning for its ties to local culture is Toon Link, which currently operates with an attractive black and white livery.

U definitely stands for University, and there are a wealth of Uni-based brand names past and present. I am going to lead with Unibus as this is the most widely used, featuring with Transdev York, Stagecoach Warwickshire, Stagecoach East Kent, Stagecoach West, First Bath, Notts & Derby and First Kernow. Also well used is Unilink, which has been adopted by First Scotland East in Stirling, Go South Coast in Southampton and is also being used by Nottingham City Transport. Sitting nicely with the City Linx and Local Linx names, UniLinx completes the family of brands used by Arriva in Leicester. Historically, meanwhile, Stagecoach in Lancaster has branded university services as Uni Sprint. U also stands for urban, and Urban Connect was, until recently, the name for Stagecoach's Lancashire service 125. In Elgin, Stagecoach currently use the name Urban Freedom for services where branded vehicles are equipped with bike racks.

V is a letter many will associate with well-regarded former North East independent Venture. Go North East pays tribute to this company by using its name for a number of rural routes out of Consett and Stanley. V also features in TrentBarton's portfolio, with a quartet of routes in the Derby and Burton area being branded as Villager. In Ayr, Stagecoach brands its network as Vision. More recently, V also stands for Vantage – First's name for the flagship busway service in Manchester which started in 2016.

While most coastal routes with names take inspiration from the word coast, W stands for Wave. This is a name used by Stagecoach for its core Eastbourne to Hastings route 99 and also for routes 100/101/102 which link Hastings with

BELOW: **Various long distance routes across Wales use the Traws Cymru name, including the T4 that links Cardiff and Merthyr Tydfil with Brecon, Llandrindod and Newtown. Illustrating the current livery is a Stagecoach Optare Tempo entering Merthyr Tydfil Bus Station in August 2012.**

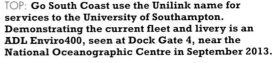

Hythe, Folkstone and Dover. Another coast-related name beginning with W is Go North East's Whey-Aye Five-O, which combines local dialect with reference to the American television series "Hawaii Five-O". Conveniently, the original number for the route this name was applied to was 50. W also stands for the Witch Way – Transdev's high-profile east Lancashire express. And W featured with the Whisky Trail branding once used by Stagecoach in Elgin.

X proved to be a difficult letter, as I didn't consider X-route -number brandings to count. Therefore, the only representation I could come up with for the letter X is the now retired Xprss brand once used in Nottingham by TrentBarton. For a present example, the closest match I could think of is Xpress as in the Tyne Tees Xpress and Wear Tees Xpress names currently used by Go North East. And another stretch is Stagecoach Hull's "Love your X" branding on the Hull to Leeds service.

Y stands for YoYo, used by Stagecoach South in Farnborough. Y also stands for Yellow School Bus, used by a number of operators although not necessarily with the crucial qualifying "yellow" part at the start of the name.

Finally, then, Z proved to be a surprisingly easy letter to work with. My favourite Z brand is TrentBarton's Zoom – a clever name for an express service. Z also stands for Zone, used for Stagecoach's Teesside services 36/37/38. In Yorkshire, First now brands Halifax to Huddersfield service 503 as Zest. And to round the article off, Zip is the former name of the previously-mentioned First Star services between Portsmouth and Waterlooville. ∎

ABOVE: **Xpress branding is used for Go North East's three express routes to Teesside. Illustrating the Tyne Tees variant is a Wrightbus-bodied Volvo B9TL, photographed in Middlesbrough Bus Station.**

BELOW: **Zip branding was used in Portsmouth for a number of years for services linking the city with Waterlooville, before giving way to a new name, The Star. Illustrating the old Zip livery in August 2013 is a Volvo B7RLE on Northern Road in Cosham.**

Trent as it was

John Robinson illustrates the vehicles of the
Trent Motor Traction Co in the NBC era.

Trent was formed on 31 October 1913
but its foundations can be traced back
to September 1909 when a company
called Commercial Car Hirers of Highgate,
London, started a bus service between Ashbourne
and Derby using a small open-sided vehicle with seats
for 22 people. A few other bus routes were developed
and in 1913 it was decided to combine with other
bus interests to form the Trent company and begin to
develop bus services over a wider area. Gradually this
area enlarged through continued expansion and the
acquisition of various independents.

Later falling under British Electric Traction, and
then National Bus Company control, the NBC years
saw significant growth when, in 1972, Midland
General was placed under Trent control, increasing
the fleet size from around 400 to 600. Also in that
year, the division of the North Western company
resulted in its Buxton and Matlock operations

ABOVE: **Trent was an early customer for the Leyland
Atlantean with the first entering service in 1959.
Between then and 1962 a total of 16 Weymann-
bodied lowbridge versions and 50 highbridge
versions with bodywork by Metro-Cammell (11),
Roe (29) and Weymann (10) were placed in service.
Roe-bodied 599 (TCH 90) is seen in the roofless
Meadow Road B garage, Derby, on 10 September
1977, a year after the disastrous fire in July
1976 which destroyed 38 vehicles including two
brand-new ECW-bodied Atlanteans which hadn't
even entered service. Remarkably, despite this
devastating loss, no mileage was lost from the
following morning's services due to the efforts of
staff and the loan of buses. When photographed 599
was the only survivor of the Roe-bodied batch. New
as 1090, it became 456 as part of a general fleet
renumbering in 1962. Towards the end of its life it
was renumbered twice in quick succession in order
to free up numbers for new Leyland Nationals,
becoming 472 in October 1976 and 599 in February
1977. Behind is one of the lowbridge Atlanteans and
behind that one of the Weymann-bodied highbridge
ones, this bodywork being distinguishable from
Roe by its slightly less angular appearance.**

ABOVE: **Looking immaculate, despite its 15 years, 382 (VCH 832), one of 15 Willowbrook-bodied Leyland Tiger Cubs new in 1961, takes on a hopelessly-uneconomic load at Matlock bus station on 13 July 1976, the day before the Derby depot fire, as it operates former North Western service 111 to Beeley, a short working of the full route to Calver Sough. The white band doesn't extend under the cab window or round the front end which was not uncommon in the application of NBC single-deck bus livery by Trent. Matlock local services are now run by TM Travel (part of Wellglade) and G&J Holmes.**

passing to Trent adding nearly 50 further vehicles, all single-deck.

The management buyout of Trent, following deregulation in 1986, resulted in the formation of parent company Wellglade; Trent continues to be in that group, one of only two former NBC operators (East Yorkshire being the other) not acquired by one of the big groups. In 1989 well-known Nottinghamshire independent Barton was purchased. It was operated as a separate entity until 2005 when the TrentBarton identity was introduced. A very strong marketing strategy, with nearly all routes now having names, rather than numbers, and each with their own distinctive livery, ensures TrentBarton continues to thrive, after a creditable 104 years operation.

This selection of pictures illustrates the diversity of vehicles operated in the NBC era.. ∎

LEFT: **The division of North Western saw its Buxton and Matlock depots pass to Trent in 1972. Subsequently, a number of indigenous Trent vehicles were transferred to them to work alongside the stock inherited from North Western. Amongst these was 180 (YRC 180), one of 20 Leyland Tiger Cubs new in 1962 with dual-purpose BET-style Alexander bodywork. It is seen in Spring Gardens, Buxton on 3 September 1973 operating former North Western service 85 to Glossop. Still wearing full pre-NBC livery, it was subsequently repainted in NBC local coach livery of red and white and lasted in service until 1977.**

ABOVE: Since 1926 Trent had been building up a network of long-distance express services resulting in coaches and dual-purpose vehicles becoming a significant part of the fleet, which featured a wide variety of chassis and body types. 55 (ACH 55B) was one of five Leyland Leopards with Harrington Grenadier bodywork which entered service in 1964 and was, perhaps, a surprising recipient of NBC coach livery (which was applied in October 1975) as depicted in this view at Derby bus station on 14 August 1976. 55 was delivered in October 1963 and was withdrawn in 1977.

ABOVE: 7 (ECH 7C), one of four Leyland Leopards with Plaxton Panorama bodies which entered service in 1965, heads out of Stockport's Mersey Square and up Rock Row in June 1973 operating service X1 from Manchester to Derby via Macclesfield, Leek and Ashbourne. It retains pre-NBC livery, although with NBC-style fleetname, and carries an attractive winged Trent motif on the front dash. It was withdrawn later that year, after just eight years in service.

ABOVE: Trent's first Daimler Fleetlines arrived in 1963, a batch of ten with Northern Counties bodywork. Subsequent deliveries, covering the period from 1965 to 1972, had Alexander (80) and, later, ECW bodies (19). 983 (HRC 483D) with Alexander bodywork, one of 11 new in 1966, is leaving Ripley for Nottingham on 26 August 1978, appearing to be freshly-repainted. Most of the Alexander-bodied Fleetlines were re-numbered in 1978 in preparation for the arrival of more Leyland Nationals, this one having originally been 483. It was sold in 1980.

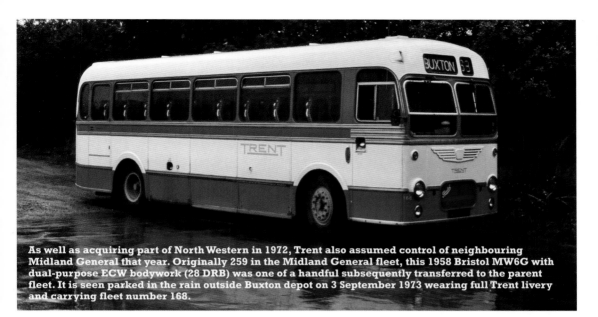

As well as acquiring part of North Western in 1972, Trent also assumed control of neighbouring Midland General that year. Originally 259 in the Midland General fleet, this 1958 Bristol MW6G with dual-purpose ECW bodywork (28 DRB) was one of a handful subsequently transferred to the parent fleet. It is seen parked in the rain outside Buxton depot on 3 September 1973 wearing full Trent livery and carrying fleet number 168.

BELOW: Also emanating from Midland General (267) was similar vehicle 118 (265 HNU), new in 1959, depicted between duties in the bus park at Matlock bus station on 13 July 1976 looking very smart in NBC local coach livery. It was withdrawn later that year.

ABOVE: A view inside Alfreton depot on 27 August 1977 sees four Bristol Lodekkas comprising, from left to right 1966 FLFs 717/8 (JNU 980/1D), both withdrawn the following June, and 1962 FSF 679 (58 JAL), acquired from Mansfield District in 1968 and withdrawn in December 1977. On the right, 1968 FLF 748 (TRB 576F) led a more charmed life, being withdrawn in November 1980 and converted into a Pizza Parlour and fast food outlet, a role it undertook for over 30 years before crossing the Irish Sea to Dublin in 2014 to continue its life as the Eco Bus Café. All were absorbed into the Trent fleet from Midland General and show that operator's route numbering system with prefix letters. The Midland General name was phased out in 1977 although was revived for a while by TrentBarton.

ABOVE: **Bristol REs first arrived at the end of 1972 in the shape of seven RELH6Ls with ECW coach bodies numbered in two batches (18-20 and 268-271). 19 (PCH 419L), stands inside Buxton depot on 3 September 1973. Another ten RELHs with similar bodywork were purchased in 1973/74, following four in 1973 with Plaxton Panorama Elite bodywork. Standing alongside is Alexander-bodied Leyland Tiger Cub 177 (YRC 177); both retain pre-NBC livery.**

BELOW: **Bristol VRs, all with ECW bodywork, were purchased by Trent between 1974 and 1981 although Midland General had commenced buying the model as early as 1969. 788 (JNN 158N), the first of four VRs new in May 1975, passes over Carlton Road level crossing outside Worksop station on 21 June that year on the lengthy service 36 from Doncaster to Nottingham, which was operated jointly with East Midland. These four VRs replaced four Roe-bodied Atlanteans which were transferred to Western National.**

ABOVE: **Upon the division of North Western in 1972, a total of 48 buses, all single-deck, passed to Trent. 295 (VDB 955), seen at Buxton Market Place on 21 June 1975, dated from 1963 and was one of nine Leyland Leopards with Alexander Y-type bodywork taken over, joining a number of similar vehicles already in the Trent fleet. The Town Hall dominates the background whilst the former North Western office, now with Trent signage, occupies one of the buildings on the left.**

ABOVE: **Although Trent had previously purchased lightweight Bedford coaches, with around 30 entering service between 1965 and 1974, it briefly turned to lightweight chassis for buses when eight Willowbrook-bodied Ford R1114s entered service in July 1976. The first, 393 (NNN 393P), stands at Buxton Market Place on 28 August that year operating service 4 to Matlock. Predictably, these vehicles had a short life with Trent, with 393 being sold in September 1980. Today services in the Buxton area are operated by High Peak, formed in April 2012 and owned 50/50 by Centrebus and Wellglade. It merged Centrebus's former Bowers operation from Chapel-en-le-Frith, and TrentBarton's Dove Holes operation.**

BELOW: **The last single-deck buses purchased in NBC days were 26 Leyland National 2s which entered service between 1980 and 1983. To reduce costs, in later years the NBC livery was simplified, dispensing with the white band. Wearing this unrelieved poppy red livery is 210 (LRB 210W), dating from 1981, seen in Buxton depot on 8 May 1985. 210 had its roof pod removed in June 1989 and passed to West Riding in May 1990.**

ABOVE: **4 (YRC194)**, a Willowbrook 003-bodied Leyland Leopard new in 1981, stands in Manchester's Chorlton Street Coach Station on 27 February 1985 operating the 4.50pm Blackpool to Birmingham (via Preston, Manchester and Hanley) National Express service 802. Trent no longer participates in National Express work, preferring to focus on local bus services. Re-registered in September 1984 with a number from a 1962 Leyland Tiger Cub bus, it was delivered as **LRR 4W** but entered service registered **PRR 4X** and was new as the team coach for Notts County FC, the world's oldest Football League Club, founded in 1862.

BELOW: **The last double-deckers purchased prior to deregulation were ECW-bodied Leyland Olympians, 24 joining the fleet between 1983 and 1985. To commemorate Trent's 70th anniversary in 1983, 705 (A705 DAU) was repainted in the traditional livery of Ayres red and cream, which had been used in various layouts from the early 1950s until the introduction of NBC livery. It is seen on the A52 Ashbourne to Derby road between Brailsford and Kirk Langley on 25 September 1983. 705 was one of ten Trent Olympians acquired by Blackpool Transport in the winter of 1996/97, continuing in service there until 2012, a slightly longer working life than with Trent and a creditable 29 years in total. The route between Uttoxeter and Derby, which includes short workings from Ashbourne to Derby (Trent's original route) is now marketed as Swift.**

An original London sightseeing tour

Fancy a quick tour of London? **Chris Drew** is ready to guide you.

"Roll up, roll up, roll up! Walk this way for the tour of a lifetime! An extravaganza that will make your jaw drop in wonder! You will pass stupendous feats of engineering and monumental amounts of masonry the like of which you will have never seen before. These objects will be paraded before your very eyes and all for no more than it costs to climb aboard this bus. And what a bus this is. This very bus could have been the star of that famous film 'Summer Holiday' if it had been built at the time. Just think, Sir Cliff himself might have sat in that very driver's seat whilst the Shadows stepped out a square on the floor where you are standing now, if, of course, the film had been made fifteen years later than it was. All this and much, much more I offer to you at such a pittance that it would be a sin to pass up the opportunity. Just sit back, relax and let us do the hard work. Let me start by showing you this.

1 "Ladies and gents. If you would like to turn your heads to the left, you will see the area called Piccadilly Circus, this is where our tour starts. This is known as the hub of London's entertainment world with theatres, restaurants and clubs on every corner. By night it is awash with neon lights that advertise just about anything you can think of. In front of you is a fountain which serves as a memorial to the Seventh Earl of Shaftesbury who did good works. Without him, some of your children might still be working up chimneys! The statue on top is regularly called Eros but I know for a fact that the sculptor, Sir Alfred Gilbert, meant him to be the Angel of Christian Charity, but somehow, that name has been lost. Anyway, he was put there in 1893 and has been a meeting point for lovers ever since. The bus you are travelling in is a one of a batch called Fleetlines. This one has the number DMS2475. My driver Charlie, who knows a thing or two about these 'ere buses has been asked by several passengers already for more details about them, after all they said, London's red buses are famous the world over. Anyway if your good selves would like to know more, write your question down on the back of a five pound note and I will pass it on to Charlie!"

2 "Hello, we seemed to have lost some people already. Everyone still here please cast your eyes to the right. This is London's most famous square on account of it commemorating Lord Nelson's victory at the battle of Trafalgar, hence Trafalgar Square. If you would like to squint into the sun, you can see the man himself standing right at the top. Up there he's some 17ft tall, which was not his real size you understand otherwise he would have kept banging his head on the yard arms. The column he's standing on puts him about 185ft above the ground. It was designed by William Railton and erected in 1839. The lions at the bottom were added by Sir Edwin Landseer nearly 30 years later. Ladies and gents, you may have noticed that we have swapped buses and indeed, somebody has stolen part of the roof. Things like this will happen now and then and is nothing to be alarmed about! We are now sitting inside an Arriva Metrobus which once worked in Hong Kong. It's a more modern bus, although to me it doesn't seem too much different from the last one but Charlie is nodding his head furiously so I guess it must be."

3 " 'Apples a pound, pears, bananas..' is just one of the many quaint street cries one may have heard in the heyday of Covent Garden. Nowadays it's a very trendy place, full of coffee shops and clothes emporiums with buskers juggling this or playing that at every turn. Back in the time when it was really a market, before the move to Nine Elms, it was London's premier place to buy fruit and veg and had been for 300 years. The name was originally Convent Garden which came from the monks of Westminster Abbey to whom it belonged. The area as it is now was put together by the Fourth Duke of Bedford who asked Inigo Jones to design a church for the west side of the market. The Duke didn't want to spend much money on the church so asked for it to be like a barn. Jones said 'It would be the handsomest barn in Europe'. That church is St Paul's church and I hope you can find time to come back and see it later. The surrounding streets are also well known for theatres and of course the Royal Opera House which is tucked away to the east of the square. Our bus this time is a real treat. This is one of a select batch of AEC Regal IV RFW-class coaches bought in the early 1950s to run tours just like the one we're on. If you care to count, there are more panes of glass than there are seats. And if you like to learn more about this bus and the many others that have plied their trade on the streets of

London, don't forget that London Transport also has it's museum in the corner of the Gardens with what is recognised as one of the best collections of buses, trams, trains, trolleybuses and everything that goes with it, to be seen in this country."

4 "You will be pleased to know that we are now leaving the Strand. This is one of the very few places in the world where, if you make your mind up to go there, you will be given a piece of fruit, as in the old music hall song 'Let's all go down the Strand, 'ave a banana!' In the middle of the road you can see a plinth with a bronze griffin on its top. The griffin has always been the heraldic beast of the City of London and this one marks the point where we enter its boundary. From here we can look forward down the entire length of Fleet Street, once the hub of London's newspaper industry and named after the river that flows underneath it on its way to the Thames. As we traverse along you might care to note that Dr Johnson's house is on the left in Gough Square. He said 'if one is tired of London, one is tired of life' and how true that is. To the right is one of Wren's most beautiful churches, St Bride's. Our bus for this part of our journey is FRM1. This is the only rear engined Routemaster to have been built although know-it-all up in the bow says there were to have been some more but it was Friday afternoon and the coffee had run out and, well, you can guess

the rest. Charlie says we are lucky to be able to use it so sit back and relax."

5 "Ladies and gentle persons, may I ask you to keep your voices down at this point. Don't panic; it's just that Charlie up front has, well shall we say, eh borrowed this bus without the knowledge of the owners. What you will notice almost immediately is that there is no sound coming from an engine. This is because we are now cooking on electric. We are now inside the City of London, the square mile as it's known. If you look to your right, you will see Sir Christopher Wren's masterpiece, St Paul's Cathedral. Notice the colour of it. That's because the stone comes from Portland in Dorset and several years ago, it was cleaned of all the soot and grime it had been gathering since it was started in 1675. The view of it from here has vastly improved over the past few years due to the removal of a railway bridge. Oh yes, the bus. Well it's one of London's fleet of what has been called the New Routemaster. Charlie and I think it should have a name of its own so it can be measured against other buses in its own right. If anybody on board has any ideas for a name, maybe they can let Charlie know at the end of the tour."

6 "This is the Mansion House. The official residence of the Lord Mayor of London, a ceremonial position and not to be confused with the Mayor of London which is purely a political position (isn't it just!). He resides on the other side of the Thames and we will pass that establishment later. Just as an interesting

point. Did you know that the Thames was the first object in London to be given a name by the Romans? Anyway, this is the view the Lord Mayor gets to watch the procession named after him. It's a good view as well. To the left is the Bank of England founded in 1694. Straight ahead is Sir Thomas Gresham's Royal Exchange building and just poking into the corner is the Stock Exchange where the jobbers and brokers operate in a permanent frenzy. Our steed for this small part of the tour is easily as recognisable as any of the architecture you will see today and of more use than some it. Anybody wants to hazard a guess as to what this bus is. Yes, you sir, yes, you with the does-he-mean-me-look-on-your-face … correct it is a Routemaster, a real Routemaster at that, one of thousands that have been wearing out the tarmac around the London for almost 50 years. We shall call it RM1163."

7 "Ladies and gentlemen, I present to you, Tower Bridge. One of the Victorian wonders of London. It's one of those strange objects that does what it was designed to do and looks like a work of art doing it. Built

by Barry and Jones, the well known Welsh half back line up, it was finished in 1894. The Gothic towers hide a steel framework which can be seen if you care to go on one of their splendid tours. Its centre span is made up of two drawbridges which rise to let shipping through into the Pool of London. There is a funny story that was once told to me about this bridge. Apparently, in December 1952, driver Albert Gunton, with his bus under him and passengers behind, leapt a gap in a bus not unlike this one; RT793 was its number if I remember correctly. Well, as he was crossing the bridge, it began to rise. What could he do? I'll tell you. He dropped a gear, put his foot to the floor and managed to jump the gap landing safe and unruffled on the other side. Don't worry folks; Charlie up front ain't into flying yet. Tell the truth, he hasn't even passed his driving test!"

only had planning permission to be there for one year, but was so successful and so well built that its life was extended for several more years. It's become one of London's top tourist attractions but you still wouldn't get me up there. I get nose bleeds if sit upstairs on the bus for too long. The bus we're using here Charlie tells me is an Alexander Dennis type Enviro200. Sounds more like the name of someone who invented a cure for the common cold, but Charlie assures me that these are 'state of the art' buses, whatever that means. If you look to your left you will see the South Bank complex. Maybe that's what he means by state of the art!"

8 "Ladies and gentlemen, kindly stay seated as we are going through the Blackwall Tunnel which links the metropolis of Stratford in the north to the sea-faring area of Greenwich to the south. As we leave the southern portal, you may just clap your eyes on the Millennium Dome. Fantastic or folly? I leave you with your own thoughts. One thing worth taking into account though....is....well...it was built on the site of the old South Eastern Gas Works and it's been held up by hot air ever since! I would like to thank Harris Bus at this point for the use of their excellent Optare Excel, quite comfy really."

9 "We are now at the Millennium Wheel or the Eye. Whatever you wish to call it, it really is a beautiful piece of engineering. Did you know? Originally it

10 "We have just crossed Westminster Bridge and if you care to glance to your left you will see The Houses of Parliament. Officially it should be called the New Palace of Westminster but that sounds more like a variety theatre ... anyway, this was originally the site of Edward the Confessor's principle royal residence and lasted as such until Henry VIII. It had been used for a meeting place for a parliament for many years but was to be lost to a fire in 1834. The present pile you see in front was started in 1840 and took 20 years to complete. It was designed by Sir Charles Barry and A W Pugin in a Gothic style to stay in keeping with Westminster Abbey just across the road. It's seen trouble in its life, both inside and out. In 1941 the House of Commons was destroyed by a bomb but even before that, it was found that

the stone used for facing the building was not man enough and crumbled away due to acid pollution in the London atmosphere. As we pass the main gate we can see everything in black and white. Let me assure you that even if we were seeing it in colour, it would still be black and white! That nice Duple 425 was Britain's answer to the Porsche racing car and it belongs to the Metropolitan Police Brass Band and they have lent it to us for a quick once around the courtyard. I do hope they keep to the speed limit. Anyway, it's a long way from those tatty old green Bedford prison buses they used to have."

11 "Whitehall, Whitehall, this is Whitehall, named after a palace which used to stand here. The only part left now is the Banqueting House, yet another building designed by Inigo Jones. Nowadays, Whitehall is better known for its government offices and was, some think still is, the administrative centre of the country. I have heard a rather more pleasant description of it. That being that Whitehall was the high street of the Commonwealth and as such, had no equal. Charlie is just going to stop and turn the lights down outside to show you the magnificence that is the Cenotaph. This has played host to Remembrance Services for over 90 years now. This is not the original mind you, that was a wood and plaster effort. When it was opened, it was immediately covered in wreaths and by public demand it was replaced by the Portland stone cenotaph you see before you. In a few seconds Charlie will turn up the lights, do a 'one-eighty' and our Enviro400 will then do a sharp left into Downing Street, not a manoeuvre normally allowed, but we have gained special permission just for you."

12 "Please keep your seats. I'm sorry it has become so crowded but apparently not only does the prime

minister want to get on and look at the technology that has suddenly appeared inside our bus, but also a herd of press-men with TV cameras as well. We did promise you a tour to remember and it's not always that the PM joins us. While we are waiting for the sherry reception to move on, let me tell you more. Not exactly a palace, number. 10 Downing Street has been the official residence of the prime ministers of this country since 1732 when Sir Robert Walpole was offered it by George II. Good, they're leaving. Let's take our bus, a Leyland Atlantean I'm informed, which has been fitted out this way by the City of Salford University, and move on before they see we've gone."

13 "Not satisfied with meeting the PM, we've managed to wangle some tickets for a party, at Buckingham Palace. Through the use of a little-known split in the space-time continuum situated 14 paces south of the bridge in St James's Park, we have been able to go back to her majesty the queen's 60th birthday party. We have gone back to 1986. Did I hear someone ask about the time-line being broken? Don't worry; our specially-designed Leyland Olympian has been fitted with a buffer against any ravages that might befall the universe as we know it.

What's that? No, madam, I'm afraid your hair will still be grey when you get off the bus, some things are actually impossible. Just before we enter the palace, a few details about the building itself. It was built in 1703 for the Duke of Buckingham, hence the name, if you wondered. It passed to the monarchy in the reign of Queen Victoria and has been the principle home of the sovereign ever since. As you get off the bus, please remember the number of it, L45, as on your return we don't want you being zapped back to a different time zone, thank you."

14

14 "Here's a treat. We dragged this old girl out of retirement just for you. You've met the PM and the queen, and in a reference only older passengers will understand I have the pleasure of telling you that this bus once belonged to a Prince! Marshall your thoughts please as you look left at the area known as Speaker's Corner where anyone can exercise his or her right of free speech without hindrance except from passing hecklers. To your right you can see the splendour that is Marble Arch. This stands at the western end of Oxford Street and originally was designed by John Nash in 1828 as an entrance to Buckingham Palace, bit of a long way for the milkman's horse to go, I hear you say. Well it did stand nearer the palace but was moved to its present position in 1851 and was closed to traffic in 1908 and is nowadays only opened for the King's Troop Royal Horse Artillery. On the Edgware Road side of the junction stands the site of Tyburn Tree, London's former home of execution and was used as such from 1196 continuously until 1783 whence the dirty deeds were transferred to Newgate. Just as an extra piece of info. The saying 'To go west' meaning to die, comes from the direction a prisoner would have to travel from Clink Street jail to their place of execution at Tyburn, but we are not going to hang around here any longer."

15 "Regent Street, one of London's most popular shopping areas. Constructed by John Nash, (there's that name again) in 1820-23 as part of a boulevard to connect the Prince Regent's house near St James's Park and the newly-acquired property of Regent's Park. Now, we are going to break from the usual tour and form a walking bus. This is because we have been given the opportunity to walk through time. For today, and today only, we can view the history of bus travel in London from the present day back to the Victorian age as we move through the crowds down Regent Street from Oxford Circus to our starting point at Piccadilly Circus.
"We hope you have enjoyed this unique tour!" ∎

15

Yorkshire 30 years ago

Tim Carter travels back in time to Yorkshire in the late 1980s, when Britain's bus industry was in transition thanks to privatisation and local bus service deregulation.

ABOVE: **One unexpected effect of deregulation was the appearance of ex-London Routemasters in towns and cities around Britain. East Yorkshire Motor Services operated Routemasters in Hull, and painted them in its traditional dark blue and primrose.**

BELOW: **United Auto converted this Bristol RE to open top for operation in Scarborough, and it passed to East Yorkshire when it took over United's Scarborough business in 1986. It is seen in Bridlington in the summer of 1988, repainted in East Yorkshire blue. This bus survives in preservation.**

ABOVE: **Scarborough Skipper was the name given to minibuses which United introduced to the town in 1986. This is a Mercedes-Benz L608D with 20-seat Reeve Burgess conversion, heading for Weaponness.**

BELOW: **Applebys operated local services in the Scarborough area and these included a summer sea front service, here being run by a former Southend Corporation Daimler Fleetline CRL6/33 with Leyland engine and Northern Counties body.**

ABOVE: **Yorkshire is an area of incredible diversity, and in the north there are attractive market towns such as Guisborough, where a United Auto Leyland National 2 pauses on its way from Middlesbrough to Whitby on service X56 in August 1987, a few months before the National Bus Company business was privatised. United was bought by Caldaire Holdings later that year.**

ABOVE: **Yorkshire Coastliner was the name used by NBC's West Yorkshire Road Car Company for limited-stop services from Leeds to Whitby, Filey, Scarborough and Bridlington via York and Malton. This Leyland Olympian was one of seven new in 1985 which had ECW bodies with 71 coach seats in place of the normal 77 bus seats. The location is Vicar Lane bus station in Leeds. The buildings still stand, but the site is now a car park.**

ABOVE: **As well as being served by Yorkshire Coastliner, Filey, Scarborough and Bridlington were connected by a route operated by Primrose Valley Coaches whose fleet in 1989 included this ex-West Midlands PTE Daimler Fleetline, still carrying its PTE fleet number, 4327, above the driver's side window. Primrose Valley had what might be described as an early attempt at route branding on this bus. The lettering above the front wheel reads: "Daily service operating from Reighton Sands, Primrose Valley and Blue Dolphin Holiday Parks to Filey, Scarborough & Bridlington." Nice idea; but did anybody actually notice?**

BELOW: **Harrogate attracted some new operators in the period following deregulation. One of these was Harrogate Independent Travel, whose fleet included three fairly rare Leyland Swifts with 37-seat Wadham Stringer Vanguard bodies. They were new in 1987 and were registered in London by Arlington, the dealer which supplied them. Harrogate Independent Travel served the town from 1987 to 1989 when it was bought by the AJS Group. AJS was the town's main operator through its Harrogate & District company, which had taken over the former West Yorkshire business in the area.**

ABOVE: **The big operator in West Yorkshire was Yorkshire Rider, the former PTE bus operation. Its fleet included small buses with Micro Rider fleetnames, as seen on an Optare CityPacer in Leeds. The stylish CityPacer was built on a MAN-VW LT55 light truck chassis. The company's 1987 intake of small buses also included Mercedes-Benz 811Ds and MCW Metroriders.**

BELOW: **Most Yorkshire Rider buses were double-deckers. This 1988 Leyland Olympian was allocated to Wakefield and was unusual in having a lowheight Northern Counties body. It was an ONCL10/1RZ with Cummins L10 engine and ZF gearbox.**

BELOW: **Ivy Travel of Huddersfield was a coach operator which also ran buses for a short time, as illustrated by a former Crosville Leyland National on its route between Huddersfield and Wakefield. Its bus operation was taken over by Caldaire in 1989.**

ABOVE: **Caldaire invested heavily in new buses, and was a major user of the Leyland Lynx. This is a Lynx II, in Wakefield bus station in the cream and green livery of Yorkshire Buses, a trading name for Yorkshire Woollen.**

BELOW: **This Caldaire Leyland National in Bradford's impressive Interchange, also operated by Yorkshire Woollen, has Yorkshire Heckmondwike as its fleet name. It had been new to Yorkshire Woollen in 1977. This photograph was taken 10 years later.**

ABOVE: **Tom Jowitt Travel operated buses in the Barnsley area until 1990 when it sold out to Yorkshire Traction, which reformed the business under the Barnsley & District name. The TJT fleet was made up largely of second-hand buses such as this former Western SMT Leyland Leopard which was 14 years old when photographed in 1989.**

ABOVE: **The extra wheel on this South Yorkshire PTE Doncaster Dennis Dominator is supposed to enhance the representation of a stylised steam locomotive which is advertising Childrens World, a shop in Rotherham. At a quick glance it makes the bus look like a twin-steer model. New in 1982, the Dennis has an Alexander RH 78-seat body. A Roe-bodied Atlantean stands alongside.**

BELOW: **The South Yorkshire PTE pioneered the operation of articulated buses in Britain in 1980. It ran MANs and Leyland DABs. The most successful of the artics were 13 Leyland DABs delivered in 1985, one of which is seen on the City Clipper service two years later. The City Clipper circulated around central Sheffield.**